Museums
& the Community
in West Africa

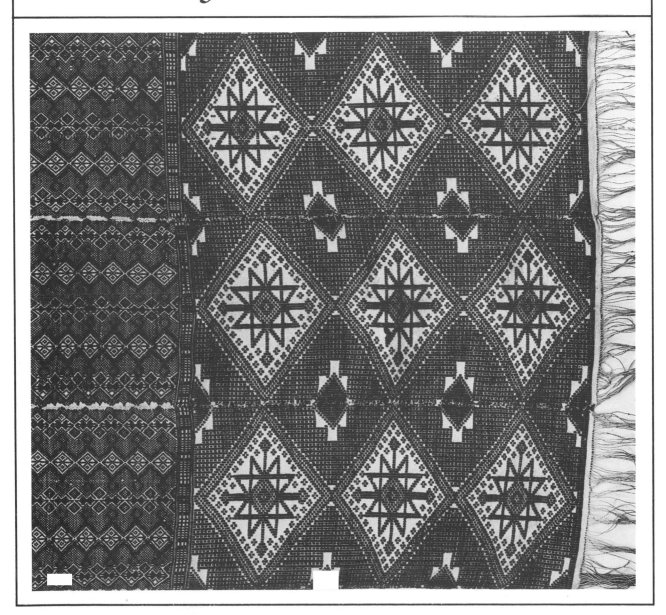

Museums & the Community in West Africa

Edited by

CLAUDE DANIEL ARDOUIN & EMMANUEL ARINZE

Published on behalf of   Smithsonian Institution Press
The West African Museums Programme   WASHINGTON
in association with   James Currey
The International African Institute   LONDON

© 1995 West African Museums Programme
All rights reserved

Published in the United States of America
by Smithsonian Institution Press

ISBN 1–56098–611–5

Library of Congress Catalog Number 95–68002

First published in Great Britain
by James Currey, London

Typeset in 11/13pt Bembo by Opus 43, Cumbria
Printed in Britain by Villiers Publications, London N3

Contents

PART II

Foreword

Museums as institutions of cultural importance should be part of the community they serve. They should be responsive to the needs of the community, and the museums and the community, both working together, should effectively contribute to the growth and development of the community. In the various programme actions that are aimed at the preservation of the cultural heritage of the community, the focal responsibility falls more on local museums than on centrally-controlled national museums. Therefore, to realise efficient museum development, there is a need to harmonise the establishment and running of local museums with that of national museums.

In recognition of this, the West African Museums Programme, with its object of stimulating and fostering the establishment and development of museums in the sub-region, felt concerned that adequate attention has not been given to the place and role of museums in the various countries. To address this issue WAMP decided to organise in Lomé, Togo, a symposium on local museums in West Africa. Professionals were invited from museums in the sub-region to discuss local museums and to formulate proposals and strategies for the establishment of such museums.

The symposium addressed a wide range of topics and subject areas, covering infrastructures for local museums, security, training, archaeology and local museums, local museums and traditional technologies, cultural inventories and opinion surveys for local museums, and the legal framework for independent local museums. In addition, various cases of local and community-based museums were studied. Such case studies included Pobe Mengao in Burkina Faso, Sikasso and Gao in Mali, Aneho in Togo, Zaranou and Bonoua in Côte d'Ivoire, the Ghana National Cultural Centre in Kumasi, the Ziguinchor independent museum project in Senegal, and the Iles Eotile museum project in Côte d'Ivoire.

A total of thirty-eight participants from twelve countries actually took part, including the late Herbert Ganslmayr, member of the Advisory Committee of ICOM.

The symposium, in addition to begetting this publication, is seen as a contribution to a process whose impact will be felt throughout the sub-region over a period as museums continue to develop and formulate policies that will make them more responsive to the aspirations and needs of their communities. Publication comes several years later. However, we believe that the issues and problems that were discussed and addressed in 1985 are still relevant and present today in the museums and countries of the sub-region.

WAMP recognizes the hospitality and support of the government and people of Togo, and of the personnel of the Musée national du Togo in making the symposium a success.

Acknowledgements

The editors would like to thank the Ford Foundation for enabling the West African Museums Programme's workshop on 'Museums and the Community' to take place and the papers to be published in this volume; Dr John Mack, Keeper, Department of Ethnography, the British Museum, for permission to use photographs from the British Museum collection; and Dr Philip Ravenhill, Chief Curator, and Amy Staples, Archivist, the National Museum of African Art, Washington, DC, for permission to use photographs from the National Museum of African Art's Eliot Elisofon Photographic Archives, Smithsonian Institution.

Introduction

PHILIP L. RAVENHILL

It seems somehow appropriate that my thoughts about the genesis of the 1985 Lomé conference devoted to the topic of local museums in West Africa are being written as I sit on an Air Afrique flight from New York to Dakar. From 1982 to 1987, during frequent flights between Abidjan and various West African capitals, I found much of my time was spent either in anticipating conversations with museum colleagues I was to meet or in reflecting on the discussions that we had had on a wide range of topics that revolved around the future of museums in West Africa.

In 1983 and 1984 the topic of creating museums in towns or villages far from the national capital – hence 'local' museums – was a recurrent topic of conversation not only with museum colleagues but also with newly elected mayors, members of community organisations, teachers, officials in different government Ministries, and ordinary citizens. Some of the most interesting discussions took place with people who had already created or cared for museums in small towns and villages where one would not ordinarily have thought a museum could be found. It was clear that different models of museums were being contrasted, and that the inherited model of a single 'national museum' was increasingly found to be inadequate. It was also clear that it would be a good idea to organise a regional conference in order to discuss the experience of existing local museums, to analyse problems that related to their legal status, to consider ways in which museums in a given country might share resources and responsibilities, and above all to raise issues for a future in which museums would be better distributed throughout the nation.

From its beginnings in 1982 the West African Museums Project (now West African Museums Programme) had sought to facilitate new museum programmes conceived directly by museum staffs in response to the challenges that they themselves perceived and articulated. One

1

of the very first initiatives for which the Project obtained funds[1] was the textile collecting and research project conceived by the Musée national of Mali. This successful research and collecting mission became the basis of the regional workshop on textile conservation that the project organised in Bamako in 1984 in collaboration with ICCROM – the International Centre for the Study of the Preservation and Conservation of Cultural Property.[2] This workshop, which brought together twenty-two museum professionals from 12 West African countries, had the additional benefit of creating a forum of exchange between West African museum professionals. In French and English, or combinations of both, museum professionals were able to talk of their experiences and share their dreams. The project became a facilitator of this dialogue and responded to it.

Having been privileged to learn first-hand about the local museum experimentation that was occurring throughout West Africa, I was able to invite 15 people to Lomé to debate the topic together. Unfortunately I fell ill and was unable to attend. Claude Ardouin, then director of the Musée national of Mali and now the director of WAMP, and Emmanuel Arinze of the National Museums of Nigeria, co-hosted and chaired the conference in my absence. The role of the facilitator – to make it possible for others to do things that otherwise might not be done – was perfectly achieved: the conference was run by those most concerned. Many topics were discussed. Most of them are represented here. I have chosen to let them speak for themselves. It is not my role nor is it my desire to explain the interest of the various topics. It is sufficient to say that this volume bears witness to an on-going dialogue between African museum professionals who are passionately concerned for the future museums of their respective countries and who care enough to share their ideas and visions.

The West African Museums Programme has always been an exponent of dialogue and exchange. From the beginning it has seen itself as an intellectual partner and a humble facilitator, taking advantage of its connections to make new visions and new approaches possible in the museums of West Africa.

Notes

1. The West African Museums Project was initially funded by the Ford Foundation, through its West African office, based in Lagos, Nigeria. In its first phase the project did not itself administer funds directly; rather, it directed funding requests to the Ford Foundation. Subsequently, funding was obtained from the Ford Foundation which allowed the project to allocate funds directly.
2. Cf. Philip L. Ravenhill, 'The past and the future of museology in sub-Saharan Africa', ICCROM Newsletter 13 (1987), 34-6.

PART

I

1 The Creation & Survival of Local Museums

ALPHA OUMAR KONARE

Most of the ideas that I shall touch on are in fact questions. Yet I am certain of one thing: we who work in museums and the cultural heritage must question the options we have hitherto accepted as to what a museum ought to be. It is vital to raise the problem of museums if we are not to become irrelevant. Every time the question is raised we hear it said that museums are foreign institutions, that they are not part of our culture, even though we used to have structures that could be regarded as places where things were conserved. In the great debate on the role and place of museums we must indeed accept that our participation is not clearly defined.

Starting from our national culture and history, we must think carefully about the most suitable means of preserving our cultural heritage. We feel that there is only one answer: to be in close contact with our culture and history. No one else will do it for us. We have no choice but to take a long, hard look at ourselves, for otherwise we shall be condemned to applauding others and feeling left behind every time some new idea appears.

If we look at the whole story of museums, in most countries, especially the francophone ones, doubt persists, even though there are some grounds for satisfaction. We doubt ourselves, faced with the enormity of the task to be accomplished, though we lack the courage to admit it to ourselves. Everyone wants to find the solution but, deep down, we wonder whether we are not engaged in a rearguard action. If a survey were to be conducted we would surely discover that young people do not know where the museums are, and do not visit them.

These museums contain objects that no longer bear any relation to the living culture. Yet they ought to take account of what currently concerns people. It is very difficult to use objects that are no longer part and parcel of the people's culture to enhance cultural awareness. Something which does not interest people will never be able to move

Figure 1.1
Elaborate
sword
blade,
Ghana
*(Photo:
British
Museum)*

5

Figure 1.2 Cloth from upper
Senegal (*Photo: British
Museum*)

them. We must not lose contact with reality. There are institutions that
have lost all contact with the living culture. Our national museums
now contain nothing but objects that have lost all function. By that I
mean that they are no longer part of the everyday culture of the people.

That leads us to an objective critique of our museums. But before
we attempt it we must look at ourselves. This contradiction could lead
us to talk of cultural suicide, but I will not go that far. In our museums
or conservation structures we must do what we have failed to do in our
schools and universities: open them up to those who are really the
repositories of our national cultures. What emerges from the current
debate on schools and universities is that these institutions are inappropriate because they are closed to those who possess the real
knowledge, the true culture.

It is not possible to separate local museums and national museums,
and, politically, there should be no dichotomy between the two.
There is a global practice of museums with a local aspect and a national
aspect. They are not two distinct, separate institutions. If we can
manage to maintain a global museum policy in each country, then local
and national museums can be integrated into the same network. That is

vital but we need to take precautions by setting out museum policies.

It must be clear that we are conserving objects not for their own sake, but for mankind in relation to man and society. If we pay more attention to the objects than to man and society we shall conserve nothing. An object cannot be conserved outside man or outside society.

A national museum may very well conserve nothing but functionless objects, if there is no further reason why they should be retained in a local museum. The role of a national museum may indeed consist in being a home for objects when they cease to be in cultural use. Objects conserved in the conventional way, European-style, can be kept in national museums. National museums may be conceived as places where the various cultures mix, where perhaps the identity of the countries of tomorrow will be created. Enormous efforts need to be made to show how the new community is created. In this way local museums take part in promoting cultural awareness in the country, while the national museum conserves objects that have lost their function. The local museum is anchored in a local culture, while national museums see things at the level of several cultural groups.

A local museum has a variety of roles. In the first place a repository for objects, it is also a documentation and educational centre open to research. It is not a place where objects are simply piled up and accumulated, but the place that holds most information about our cultures. Material circumstances in our countries compel us to set out the functions of the local museums very carefully. It is not a matter of setting up small-scale national museums. Key features of a local museum are field research and its role in promoting awareness and education, while at the same time remaining a place where objects are conserved.

Next, it must be stressed that the museums of the future cannot be conceived for a minority of foreigners or intellectuals but must be for the majority of the population. The whole of the heritage must be our concern: the physical and natural heritage (the framework in which the history of man unfolds), as well as the artistic heritage. In Africa no object is totally devoid of meaning. A religious object cannot be looked at apart from the religion and the ceremonies with which it is associated. It is vital to develop a global vision of the heritage. The heritage must be taken in its totality. This is all the more important because in our countries those who are concerned with the past and those who are concerned with museums are the same people.

Another vital aspect is that museums must be related to our own culture. And the first issue that arises is what units should be conserved.

Figure 1.3 Face mask of wood, Yaure people, Côte d'Ivoire (*Photo: Franko Khoury, National Museum of African Art, Washington DC*)

7

Figure 1.4 Mask, front view, Mali (*Photo: British Museum*)

Naturally, to conserve an object means preserving it, but it also means keeping the language that surrounds it. An object is conserved when its continued use is assured. In fact everything that remains in the hands of the people and is used by them is truly protected and preserved. Custom and tradition see that such things are protected. What is not used has no life and so is not conserved. We must think about this notion of conservation, for only when we have defined it will we be able to grasp the problem of museums.

Another issue is museum policy. It is often proclaimed that creating a museum is our duty to future generations. But that is simply a pose: a museum is about safeguarding the cultural heritage for ourselves, it is vital for our own physical and moral well-being.

One approach to museum policy is essential if there is to be a vision of what it is we want to achieve: programming, whether it be for a national museum or a local one. A general strategy is needed, an overall view, a national policy. Nothing should be undertaken without proper programming. That means we must have a vision of the local museum we are going to create. We have often made mistakes: in our enthusiasm we have set up museums without asking ourselves the basic questions that ought to have been part of an overall strategy. But there has never been any co-ordination of museum policy at the national level, still less at the local level. It is thus essential that there should be such a national policy, while taking care to avoid bureaucratisation, which is anti-cultural.

Everyone wants to promote local museums. But why promote them? Fundamentally, the idea is linked with that of decentralisation, on which we place such stress in the area of culture. A local museum is the base and, furthermore, it costs less than a national museum, with the heavy investment the latter involves. It responds better to the problems and concerns of ordinary people. Local museums may help to accelerate the spread of national awareness. They take part in the creation of culture. Until a new culture has been created, an old one cannot be conserved. And a local museum is clearly one of the best places where culture can be updated.

There cannot be a local museum policy without reference to the national museum. In future, the national museum (several, if the country has the means) may be regarded as a motor for all the museums. The national museum may be an example, with all the necessary infrastructure, and provide an impetus by fulfilling a number of roles. In Mali, for example, efforts are highly concentrated; there is a big national museum, as local museums lack the means to support a

Figure 1.5 Collander made of
palm fronds, Ghana
(*Photo: British Museum*)

proper infrastructure, and the national museum is in a sense a laboratory for the local museums (see also Chapter 15). The national museum
may also become a database for local museums, recording the heritage
and seeing to its inventory.

What are the limits of local museums? Their only limits are those of
the community. Any object used by a community should come within
the purview of the local museum. A museum has no other limit than
that which the community sets it. Care must also be taken not to stifle
the culture. For example, in some religious cults there are objects that
must not be seen by women. Such objects should not be on public
display.

As regards the form of museums, there is no one particular type.
There are as many local museums as there are communities and
cultures. There are local museums in buildings, there could be some in
the open air, there may be district museums, or school museums, or

theatre museums, or travelling exhibition services, or shows which fulfil the same role. Nor should we forget the conservation role of craft villages. The best is still the dispersed one with 'monuments' scattered about, arranged along a route, with the objects remaining in fact in the hands of their owners. For one can speak of a museum only if conservation is assured without necessarily entailing the acquisition or appropriation of objects.

It is thus important to reflect on our culture, in order to arrive at a proper programme for museums. That includes staffing problems. Qualified staff need to be employed. Upgrading the museum profession must also be part of local museum policy. If there is no sustained continuity in the work of those who look after the cultural heritage, then it will serve no purpose. The role of curators is important, but so is that of technicians.

We must also be open to traditional knowledge, the knowledge of the people, of notables, men of culture. The local museum cannot be just the concern of the curator. We will not succeed in getting any structure properly established without looking at our history.

2 *The Relationship between Local Museums & the National Museum*

BABA MOUSSA KONATE

In most countries in West Africa the need to set up museums to offset the paucity – and also the observed uneven distribution – of institutions responsible for protecting the cultural heritage has become a political imperative. But the widely expressed willingness of governments to create museums encounters enormous difficulties when it comes to putting it into practice, for the projects proposed often require considerable expenditure. It is therefore important to reflect on the definition of appropriate strategies for the implementation of museum policies. Seen from this angle, local museums – surprising, given their relative novelty – constitute one of the most appropriate solutions.

An examination of museum development strategies brings out two possible methods. [1]

1. One consists in creating 'autonomous' museums endowed with a range of technical structures required for them to function. It is extremely difficult to implement such a method in low-income countries. It requires large sums of money which the public does not see as well spent if spent on a museum.

2. The other consists in setting up a network of museums in which a single well equipped museum acts as technical co-ordinator of the activities of other museums. What is required then is for that museum to be equipped with the technical skills which will be used to give impetus to the other museums. This method has the advantage of being less expensive, in so far as all the other museums will be able to get going with simple infrastructures. For that reason it appeals to low-income countries anxious to establish museum institutions. Therefore in the following pages we shall examine the role that a well equipped museum might play in relation to other museums with limited technical resources.

11

What relations would then exist between the two types of museums? How would the status of the former in relation to the latter be defined in such a way as not to compromise the way the latter operate? To answer these questions we may start from experience in Mali and then examine the implications of the strategy thus adopted.

Following two days of brainstorming about the cultural heritage – on 17 and 18 May 1976 – Mali set out a new policy for creating museums. Over those two days it became clear that no museum-building project would be viable until the situation of the Musée national was improved. Rehabilitation of the old national museum was thus seen as a starting point for any project to establish new museums. In other words, regional and local museums, the creation of which had been recommended by the study days, should be contemplated only after the reorganisation of the Musée national.

This principle clearly determined the general direction given to projects for creating museums in Mali. A new complex was built with French technical and financial assistance and was inaugurated in March 1982. Getting that far left major problems still to be faced: the lack of technical facilities, in terms both of skilled personnel and the equipment of the buildings, on top of the state of the collections inherited from the former museum, seriously compromised the operations of the new museum. If such was to be the fate of the Musée national, any other attempt to set up a museum, the framework of the new museum policy, would be a non-starter. It thus became urgent to agree on a plan of action based on what was needed for the proper functioning of the museum. This plan included a training element, the first phase of

Figure 2.1 Conservation laboratory for textiles (*Photo:Musée national du Mali*)

which involved providing the staff with the basic technical skills required for the development of museum activities, and an element concerned with the equipment of technical services as and when various sectors of activity developed. With such a plan the basic problems of the very existence of the museum were solved. It is striking that three years after its reorganisation the Musée national possesses four functional services, of not inconsiderable size:

1. A conservation and restoration service, with three laboratories: textiles and leather, wood, metals and ceramics.

2. A documentation service, with a photo archive, a library and a tape library.

3. An audio-visual service, including a photo unit with a photography studio and a processing laboratory, a video unit with filming and mounting equipment, and a maintenance unit for the museum's mechanical, electrical and electronic equipment.

4. An exhibition and educational service, with a unit responsible for mounting exhibitions and an educational unit.

It cannot be denied that the experience thus acquired by the Musée national is beneficial to the creation of regional and local museums. It was thus appropriate that, in accordance with the recommendation of the May 1976 sessions, the Musée national should turn towards the roles it is called upon to play in the establishment of other museums in Mali. A new experience of assistance between the Musée national and the regional museums at Gao and Sikasso began. It should be noted, however, that at the point when the project of creating the regional museum at Gao (the Musée du Sahel) was launched, the new complex

Figure 2.2 (above) Conservation laboratory for metals and ceramics: restoration of pottery (*Photo: Musée national du Mali*)

Figure 2.3 (left) Conservation laboratory for artefacts of wood: restoration of a musical instrument (*Photo: Musée national du Mali*)

13

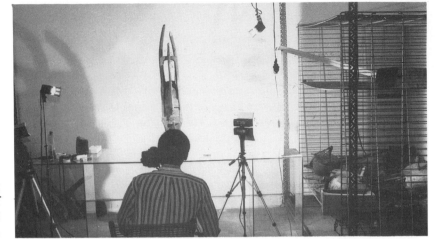

Figure 2.4 Studio for making photographic records of collections (*Photo: Musée national du Mali*)

Figure 2.5 Processing laboratory for restoration of photographic documents (*Photo: Musée national du Mali*)

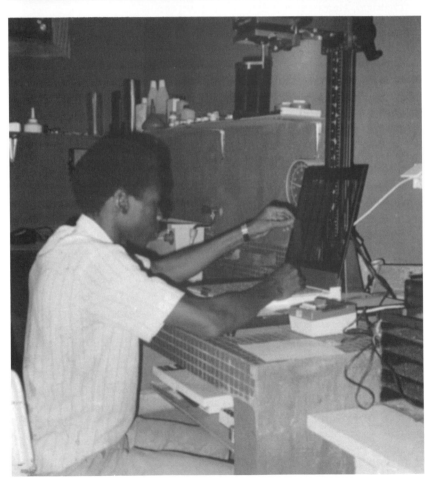

of the Musée national was yet to become operational. Because of the shortage of trained museum personnel in Mali, the exhibition conceived and realised by the Bremen Overseas Museum in the Federal Republic of Germany served as the inaugural exhibition of the Musée du Sahel. After the launching of the museum numerous technical problems arose: the services of the Musée national were approached to help find solutions to the difficulties facing the new regional museum. In the light of what happened at Gao it became apparent that the Musée national had to be involved in studying and analysing the problems associated with the regional and local museums.

The circumstances in which the Musée du Sahel came into being prevented the Musée national from becoming involved in the establishment of the Gao museum, but such was not the case with the regional museum in Sikasso. From the initiation of the project the Musée national was involved at various levels:

1. The planning of what needed to be done in the framework of setting up the museum: informing the local people, seeking out sites, training staff, building up collections and getting activities under way.

2. Technical studies for setting up the museum: the Musée national made a substantial contribution to setting out the guidelines for the architectural programme of the Sikasso regional museum (basic structure, style and building materials in relation to problems of con-servation, surface areas presently required and areas for enlargement.

3. Technical assistance in training personnel: the programme for training the staff of regional museums includes an introduction to the

Figure 2.6
Documenting museum
collections (*Photo:
Musée national du Mali*)

15

basic museum techniques of the Musée national, whose staff and technical services have a great deal to offer in this area. The practical experience achieved in this area has proved most fruitful.

4. Technical assistance in the area of museography. The Musée national did all the processing of the collections intended for the Sikasso museum (documenting collections and photographic documentation, processing of objects, etc.).

These various forms of assistance make it possible to grasp the Musée national du Mali's role in the creation of a regional or local museum. The circumstances in which the regional museums were launched – with very limited material and financial resources – mean that the Musée national is the sole source of technical back-up for the regional museums. Above and beyond the ordinary co-operative relations between museums within a single country, the assistance provided by the Musée national, in current conditions, is absolutely essential to the survival of the regional and local museums.

As things stand, it is too early to draw all the lessons from this experience. However, it already raises a number of issues which are worth looking at.

1. *Clear legal framework*. The experience described above flows from a strategic choice which derives from a museum policy. It became clear that there was a need for a clear legal framework in which relations between local museums and the Musée national countrywide could develop. Although this framework depends on how these matters are organised in each State, it is important to avoid putting up any barriers between local museums and the national museum. However, there would seem to be three possible forms of organisation:

The first is to make the national museum a central museum co-ordinating the activities of local museums. In this framework, the local museums become local outlets of the national museum. This form of organisation is burdensome especially for countries with several museums. It also has the drawback that it involves reproducing the national museum all over the country.

The second pattern is to make the national museum a co-ordinating structure for local museums. In line with this formula the national museum provides local museums with technical assistance, both at the establishment stage and when the museum is up and running. In the context of the countries of West Africa it is possible that the national museum, given its technical capacities, might give assistance to anyone in possession of cultural property who could demonstrate the need for it.

The third possibility is that local museums and the national museum both belong to a general inspectorate which lays down the relations among museums.

2. *Security problems in local museums*. If we accept that local museums will be created with a simple infrastructure, we should consider the measures to be taken to ensure the security of collections against natural disasters and accidents. It is also important to think about the role the national museum might play in helping to prevent theft from local and regional collections.

3. *The need for cooperation between local museums and the national museum*. Relations between museums can usefully be looked at as dynamic, creating feedback conditions. If the national museum provides local museums with technical assistance, it is vital that the latter should serve as outlets for the activities of the national museum at the local level. Whether they are branches of the national museum or not, local museums can play host locally to the national museum's educational teams and facilitate the establishment of co-operative relations with the local people. Museums can also exchange documents and exhibitions and make loans.

Analysis of relations between local museums and the national museum raises a host of questions which will have to be answered in terms of the reality within each country. In any event, it is desirable, whatever the context, to co-ordinate efforts to create museums by organising the available talents for the implementation of new projects. In carrying out museum policies it is important to broaden the framework of co-operation each time by involving in the realisation of projects all the talents – indeed, all the potential – that the country possesses. That should avoid repeating past mistakes whose consequences we still suffer.

1. Other strategies may exist for the establishment of museums but we feel that most of them derive from those mentioned here. *Note*

17

3 Security in Local Museums of the West African Region

SAMUEL DAYO ADELOYE

The topic of security in local museums cannot be dealt with properly unless we define what in our context is a local museum, after which we shall examine the region of West Africa in the second, or main part of this chapter, where we define security and discuss how museums of the region can cope with the security needed in the protection of the cultural property of the technologically disadvantaged region of West Africa, particularly our type of museum, located in remote and rural areas.

During the normal performance of my duties as a civil servant working for the National Museums of Nigeria, I met various local community leaders who indicated their desire not to part with their material culture for the national collection, but rather wanted to know if they could set up their own museums where their objects could be preserved and presented for their enjoyment. This is a new awakening and nothing in the constitution of Nigeria prevents such aspirants from having museums of their own once the basic requirements are met.

It is the constitutional right of a citizen to have access to education and as it is ideal to locate schools for formal education within the easy reach of all, so museums, as a vehicle of informal education, should be located as close as possible to every community. In contrast to the national museums located in large urban centres and usually a prestigious national edifice, housing collections from the various cultural groups that make up the nation, and sometimes playing down some less prolific artistic areas of the country and/or rejecting materials that are of little national historical importance, the local museum serves the local community and collects the artefacts of its cultural history. It is a small but unique institution because communities can preserve and appreciate their cultural heritage at the local level – an institutional framework which ensures the protection of cultural property and the national use of same for education and cultural purposes.

Figure 3.1 Equestrian figure of fired clay, Niger River, Mali (*Photo: Franko Khoury, NMAfA, Washington DC*)

19

Most countries of the world have different categories and tiers of museums, serving different communities and performing various functions. There are national, regional, provincial and country or city museums, the obvious difference being who is behind the establishment and funding. Since the funding of central museums is in most cases from the public treasury, the personnel, to varying degrees, are public servants who owe their first allegiance to the board of trustees rather than to the collections. There is usually no umbilical attachment of any special nature to the cultural artefacts placed under their care other than the general feeling shared within the wider national community. Sometimes the curator or the director himself may not belong to the community that owns the cultural patrimony he presides over.

In the Nigerian situation one can identify two museums that could rightly be called local in a very close and related sense. These are the Kanta Museum at Argungu in Sokoto State and the Odinani Museum in Anambra State. The former houses the collections of the Emir, which are located in the old palace. The items in these museums are of great historical importance to the emirate and its glorious past. The Emir, his chiefs and the local citizens are aware of the importance of

Figure 3.2 Three standing female figures in a beaded vest, Yoruba, Nigeria (*Photo: Franko Khoury, National Museum of African Art, Washington, DC*)

the collection to the community and its survival is a corporate concern. The Odinani museum was established through the motivation of outside forces – the Institute of African Studies of the University of Ibadan, which spends substantially to keep the museum going.

In my opinion these are the two museums which would probably meet our present definition of local museums. However, we shall consider others which share the same similarities to some extent.

National &
Local Museums

The museums at Ile-Ife, Owo, Esie, Oron and the Gidan Makama in Kano are local in the sense that the cultural artefacts housed in them originated from the locality and are kept in these museums, specially established by the central national government for the purpose of preserving and presenting the artefacts within the cultural context that produced them. The artefacts contained in these museums are either archaeological or ethnographic in nature but they belong to the people who live within the cultural areas where the objects are being displayed.

However, the local museums under consideration have the peculiarity of self-discovery and determination on the part of their founders, who belonged to the same communities with the same cultural and historical affinities, which the museums are supposed to serve. Our local museum is a corporate venture, with ownership vested in the entire members of the founding community. Irrespective of class, age, sex, religion or belief, it is a project of consensus and common will. Everybody knows or is supposed to understand the history and the contents of the museum. They are aware of the circumstances surrounding the creation, the use and the historical and cultural significance of the collections. As has been rightly stated, there is a special sentimental commitment within a community towards a museum that preserves its cultural patrimony in the cultural atmosphere and setting that created it. It is a unique feeling, a different experience from older established national, regional or provincial museums which were motivated, constructed and financed by a central government, the funding of which is usually generated from a central or sometimes external sources.

Here, then, funding of our type of museum is of significance and a major parameter for categorisation. Since the local museum is a baby of the community, the need for a central subvention may not arise, or, if it does, very minimally. The community assumes total responsibility for

Figure 3.3 Dogon wooden
Kanaga mask, Mali
(*Photo: British Museum*)

the survival and management of the collection in all its ramifications. It is everybody's business to ensure the continued existence of the entire outfit, since the loss of artefacts or heirlooms might be calamitous and of grave concern and psychological consequence to the people and their well-being. Sometimes the loss, partial or total would be abominable and might call for a special atonement. The community cannot afford the loss and its grave consequences.

It is therefore the corporate nature of the local museum, the collective concern for the security of its contents, the joint ownership of the cultural property, that make the security of the local museum – or, simply put, the required protective measures and surveillance – less cumbersome and expensive compared with large museums in urban centres. A local museum is therefore faced with lesser threats than the central national museums located in metropolitan and urban environments.

Before discussing the various threats confronting the physical existence of our local museums, I crave the indulgence to point out two significant differences of the local museums in the West African region from those in the technologically advanced countries of Europe and America. First, the artefacts located in our museums are of current sociological value. They belong to living cultures and in some cases are still venerated. This factor, as we shall see, stands to the advantage of our local museum, that is – within the so-called face to face society, where members of the community are known to each other, where there are cultural norms that regulate relationship, where people know their rights and obligations – it makes the job of providing the required protection less elaborate and expensive.[1]

Museum Security However small or financially indigent a museum, whatever and wherever its location, there is the need for security policy, which should not be assumed, and whoever is in charge should draw up procedures for the security of the museum and its contents which must be known by all. The task of encouraging community participation in and support for the museum requires a tremendous educational effort. Since there is little or no financial assistance coming from the government, the community must be prepared to bear the load. Any attempt to solicit external assistance amounts to selling the community's integrity. Government at various levels, external institutions and organisations wanting to assist the community, must embark on a mass campaign for

22

the protection of cultural property by creating general awareness and making the museum the centre of communities' cultural activities.

Cultural property protection is a primary need. Security has been seen erroneously as a reaction to the community's crime rate, whereas the essential protection needs of a museum are:

1. Good physical protection,
2. Proper object handling and storage,
3. Good climatic control,
4. Conservation,
5. Proper employee practice, i.e. enforcing professional ethics.

Figure 3.4 Head of an Oba in cast copper alloy with metal inlay, Nigeria, 18th Century
(*Photo: Jeffery Ploskonka, Gift of Joseph H. Hirshorn, NMAfA, Washington, DC*)

23

In our part of the world, therefore, cultural property protection is a primary need of our museums, especially of the under-funded museums, to:

1. Protect what community patrimony exists both within and beyond their current spheres of influence,

2. Steadfastly resist the chances of armed conflict, eroding climate, and natural disaster,

3. Follow reliable practices of identifying the primary causes of loss and preservation,

4. Pursue community legislation for the protection of local un-excavated heritage, prevention of unauthorised exports and methods for restitution,

5. Assist museum administrators in channelling tourist flows and economic activity away from unprotected properties and towards the controlled museum collection.

Responsibility and training

Museums in every stage of their development have the obligation to protect their collections from loss and damage of any sort and they have the obligation to protect their staff and their visitors as far as possible from hazards that may exist in the work, study and exhibition areas. The ideal in large museums is to create the post of security director, with a straight line of command to the museum authority; local museums with the major handicap of inadequate funding cannot afford this practice. Hence the maxim 'Security is everybody's business' is much more applicable.

The curator or keeper, whether paid or honorary, must have executive power on the issue of security and must ensure that he organises regular training in security practice, especially fire protection, for his workers in particular and for the community in general. He must mount a special campaign against bush burning, which I perceive as the greatest threat to the local museum. He must know his museum and how to take commonsense measures to protect the people, the property and the facilities. Examples of such action are closing and locking all windows and doors at night, locking away objects that need not be exposed, knowing what to do if there is fire, knowing how to summon up the whole community for action on which they have been previously briefed or how to call for fire service assistance if any is close by. It is advisable for the community to rotate among themselves the function of security officer on duty, which should be co-ordinated by the curator or keeper. The national leaders' or chiefs' interest should be kindled. The district or provincial fire service should be invited to demonstrate the use of fire extinguishers and other extinguishing agents provided at the museum. Constant security meetings should be organised where basic skills can be introduced through talks. Each meeting should end with an environmental sanitation exercise. An alarm gong should be kept on the premises for the use of the security officer on duty, and the entire community should be aware of the signals and their meanings. On the other hand, the use of a slit drum or talking drum may be more interesting and culturally relevant. However, if it is financially possible, security staff should be employed and trained to use their senses. If any consideration can be given to hiring staff for the museum at all, it should be a security guard who could combine other roles such as guide or interpreter.

Collection security

The heart of a museum is its collections. The first obligation of a museum (whatever its size) is to recognise and assume the responsibilities inherent in the possession of its collections, which are held in trust for the benefit of the present and future citizens of the community.[2] All museums collect, preserve, and present artefacts on which they constantly carry out research, but the most challenging aspect of the job is to be able to account for a given object when required to do so. Many losses have occurred due to bad record-keeping and lack of inventory control. All museums around the world are guilty of bad record-keeping in some degree. However, many of them have woken up to this problem and have taken the necessary care to normalise and up-date their documentation systems. Some have even resorted to computerisation.

It is the primary responsibility of the curator or keeper to ensure adequate documentation of all objects in the collection. There must exist at least a record of every object, and the record must contain the following fields:

1. Accession (catalogue) number,
2. Name of the object (local),
3. Function or use,
4. Material,
5. Mode of acquisition,
6. Brief description,
7. Location.

Figure 3.5 Modern Asante container with lid of cast copper alloy, Ghana (*Photo: Franko Khoury, Gift of Ministry of Trade and Tourism, NMAfA, Washington, DC*)

If financially possible, a photograph of each object or at least a sketch should accompany its record. The essence of this record is to facilitate retrieval within the museum at any given time or in the event of loss through theft. In addition to the inventory records, there should be continuous physical inspection of the objects. This helps to detect theft as soon as it occurs. All objects coming into the museum must be identified immediately with a unique permanent number or mark.

It is advisable for descriptive records to be produced in triplicate, or at least duplicate, with each copy separately located. When there is any need for objects to be moved, adequate precautionary measures must be taken to guarantee their safety. Portable objects of high commercial value are especially vulnerable and should be specially handled or moved by responsible authority. They should not be left exposed, as that might be too tempting to the dishonest.

Environmental damage is a major threat to collections in tropical regions, especially in Africa. Ideally, irrespective of size, a museum should have a conservator on its staff but is this really practical? Nevertheless it is important that all knowledgeable members of the local museum authority or its day-to-day staff should be able to recognise and report simple damage to collections. A special arrangement should be made with the nearest larger museum having a conservator, to maintain constant or occasional survey of the collection in order to forestall damage and to treat affected objects when it occurs. A workable arrangement is to enlist the interest of teachers of chemistry in nearby secondary schools who could be given basic orientation in museum conservation.

Lighting. Although a must in any museum exhibition, lighting could be injurious to the continuous existence of an object, especially if the proper type is not employed. As recommended by UNESCO, the number of lumens of light should be reduced to lessen the effects,[3] Objects susceptible to colour fading should not receive more than 5 lumens. Different materials are able to bear different intensity of lighting but direct lighting should be avoided. When possible, also, lights should be placed outside display cases to avoid drawing dust into them.

The atmosphere holds more moisture when it is warm. The moisture content of the atmosphere dangerously affects objects in the museum. Objects composed of different materials are more prone to suffer from atmospheric change owing to the constant expansion and contraction at different rates. Chemical deterioration therefore sets in. Changes in relative humidity can be controlled through wax coating of iron objects; rice (if silica gel cannot be obtained) should be placed in showcases to absorb moisture. In storage areas, the circulation of air should be assisted, if not through air-conditioning, by ventilation ducts and fans.

Pest control is better handled by a professional conservator.

27

However, ordinary insecticides could be bought off the shelf to exterminate pests like cockroaches, moths, termites, book lice, beetles and ants. House mice,which will eat anything, should be prevented from entering storage areas. Doors and windows must be shut tight and all holes blocked as soon as they are detected. If, however, the presence of rodents is noticed they can be caught with traps or exterminated with rat poison. The entire staff and possibly informed members of the community should be educated to watch out for signs of damage from pests.

Finally, excessive handling of objects should be discouraged and any handling at all should be with care. The museums of the developed countries, particularly in Europe and America, are more prone to theft but no institution is completely immune. The fact that the large museums are aware of the danger of theft enables them to be on guard; their preparedness gives an impression of protection, and the feeling and display of effective protective measures is a deterrent to theft.

Physical security　The provision of physical security is a must in any museum, and this in itself means a wide range of integrated programmes:

1. Physical guarding,
2. Inspections,
3. Guard response procedures,
4. Inventory,
5. Property pass system,
6. 'Sign-in-sign-out' registers,
7. Personal background checks,
8. Visitors' control systems,
9. Accident procedures.
10. Evacuation procedures,
11. Damage checks,
12. Property check points.

Physical security can be provided by providing a 'bull's eye' of perimeters of defence around and inside a building. Such a perimeter could be massive, imaginative, wall-like, or merely of rope or even human eyes. It could be a glass-case perimeter or a box with lock(s) on it. The physical security is reinforced by a combination of systems – guard post, alarms, lighting, walls, etc. The outer perimeter is controlled and put under close surveillance to ensure that people do not take museum property through, except with authority, which must be verified, while the inner perimeter must be controlled to disallow unauthorised entry. Public areas must be controlled to prevent vandalism, especially from strangers and children. The community must educate its children and members to respect the museum and its contents, which are corporate property.

Theft. The museum should protect all its property, particularly the collection. Fortunately objects on display are usually better protected because of the physical barrier provided around them and because they are usually under close surveillance when the museum is opened. More theft occurs in work areas and collection storage, usually perpetrated by insiders for financial motives. Our museum is at advantage here because of the nature of the workers, their relationship to the object and the fear of being easily detected. In museums, any theft committed by outsiders usually requires the assistance of an insider. The museum staff should not be given unchecked freedom and the curator or keeper should keep a watchful eye on all.

To deter intruders from the museum at night, there should be few doors and windows, and they should be fastened internally. There should be a final exit, which must be secured with reliable locks and possibly a reinforced metal door with a heavy padlock should protect the wooden door.

Fences and gates should be high enough to serve as barriers, to vehicles in particular. It is possible for the community, working together, to provide strong enough fences for the protection of their cultural heritage. However, where the resources are not available the community could make do with dense thorny hedges. Doors and windows must be properly protected. Preferably, deadbolts should be used on doors rather than spring bolts that could be jammed. The curator must ensure that he personally checks that all doors and windows are properly locked. As resources become available with time, the access and lock system should be reviewed and updated.

Vandalism is the intentional and wilful damage or destruction of property. It is either malicious or has other motivations, such as a supposed moral obligation or religious fervour. A dirty and unkempt museum might encourage the act. Adequate measures should be taken to protect items on display, such as:

1. Good 'housekeeping',
2. Effective guarding and surveillance,
3. Encasement of tempting objects,
4. Use of physical barriers,
5. Proper public education through graphic signs.

29

Visitor guiding helps a lot, and groups should not be uncontrollable. They should be limited to a manageable size.

Communications. The following methods could be used effectively to pass information in an emergency:

1. Voice calls,
2. Hand signals,
3. Talking drum and slit drums,
4. Gongs and sounding metals,
5. Whistles,
6. Flutes and horns,
7. Bells,
8. Electric lights and flashing light signals,
9. Electronic gadgets (telephones, intercom, radio, etc.).

The community must be trained to understand signals and know how to react. Children should be educated as to the use of the communication system so as not to desensitise the community through indiscriminate application.

Weapons. It is illegal for ordinary citizens of West African countries who are not in the armed services to bear automatic weapons or firearms. However, in some cases, dane guns, spears, bows and arrows are permitted and carried by hunters and local guards. If these are legal, the night guards in the museum could carry them for self-defence. The mere sight of them is a deterrent to would-be intruders.

Fire protection Fire protection includes safety of life, fire prevention, detection, suppression and containment. Many museums lack the financial resources necessary for sophisticated fire protection systems. Good planning could meet the basic need for effective protection. The following are the initial steps to take:

1. Separate combustible materials from ignition sources.

2. Remove all unnecessary combustible materials and maintain a neat and orderly museum. Neatness is the most important factor in the prevention of fire.

3. Cut back the bush and trees outside the museum to maintain 25–30 ft (7–9 m) clearance around the building.

4. Provide adequate water for fire-fighting. If water is not readily available, keep 55 gallon (208 l) drums filled with water around the museum, with buckets. Elevated water reservoirs or tanks can provide a substantial, gravity-fed emergency water supply. Sunk wells could be very handy in rural areas.

5. Have the electrical systems evaluated by a qualified electrician.

The electrician should also provide additional power socket outlets if necessary.

6. Turn off all electrical power to the building when it is unoccupied unless this would affect the operation of the intrusion detection and fire alarm systems, if any.

7. Avoid open flames within the museum. If a fire is absolutely necessary, open flames should be located away from combustibles and in a ventilated area. Never use candle light for any purpose in the museum, especially when public power supply fails.

8. Do not introduce exhibits that might be a fire hazard into the building. Separate combustible exhibits from other exhibits.

9. Provide at least two exits from every area. Mark them clearly, keep them clear of obstructions, and practise using them.

10. Do not allow overcrowding. Control the flow of people into the building.

11. Provide a fire alarm system such as whistles, hand bells or horns both to alert the public to get out and to call the attention of the fire brigade.

12. Assign a person or people to be responsible solely for fire protection in the museum.

13. Conduct fire inspections frequently.

14. Develop a plan to deal with fire before it occurs.

15. Do not allow smoking in the museum. Provide buckets of sand at each entrance so that people can extinguish their cigarettes before entering.

16. Instruct employees what to do in case of fire, such as how to evacuate the building, how to alert the fire brigade, and how to close doors as they leave the building.

17. Avoid using combustible materials for construction whenever possible.

18. Keep flammable liquids outside and away from the museum.

Inexpensive battery-operated smoke detectors could be provided in areas of a museum that are not constantly attended if the warning sound of the detectors can be plainly heard.

Portable fire extinguishers are very effective on small fires. The extinguisher contains water, a water mixture or a powder or carbon dioxide or other gas under pressure to squirt out on to a fire. Each type of extinguisher has a special application and advantage as well as disadvantages. Buckets of water and sand placed within easy reach inside the premises could be used as substitutes. It is important to ensure that all are kept ready for use in emergency.

Fire hazards. Good 'housekeeping' and constant fire inspection do much to control fire hazards. The following habits must be inculcated if hazards are to be eliminated:

1. Avoid bush-burning within a radius of 2 km of the museum,

2. Avoid any open flame within the building, especially the use of candles when the public electricity supply fails,

3. Maintain a neat and orderly museum inside and out,

4. Keep combustible storage to the barest minimum. Special attention should be paid to storage, rooms that house machinery, car parks, workshops, kitchens, packing rooms and the like,

5. Provide suitable metal containers with tight-fitting lids, for waste paper and other refuse,

6. Take care over the storage of flammable liquids, which must be kept in labelled containers and stored well away from everything else, preferably on metal shelving,

7. Smoking should be prohibited in the museum except perhaps in specially designated areas. Do not provide ashtrays where smoking is not permitted,

8. Electrical wiring must be inspected regularly and faults rectified as soon as they are detected,

9. All electrical equipment must be properly maintained,

10. Prohibit the use of electrical appliances in the museum. If they must be used, regulate the conditions of use.

Fire detection. A good fire detection system should be in operation continuously. It is not difficult to detect fire in its earliest stages before flames develop. People are endowed with a good sense of smell and could sniff easily. Constant patrolling leads to the quick detection of fire through smell. Inexpensive smoke detectors could be installed in sensitive areas like the storage and exhibition rooms.

Fire alarm. As soon as a fire is detected the alarm should be sounded to warn people to evacuate the museum quickly and to alert those responsible for dealing with a fire. There should be a clear-cut fire alarm procedure which must be understood by everybody associated with the museum. Anybody discovering a fire must raise a voice alarm before the central alarm is sounded to summon help from the community. For an adequate supply of water for fire suppression I would recommend that a well should be sunk on the premises of the museum and, if possible, a cheap pump system should be installed to raise the water to an overhead reservoir for gravity feed.

All members of the community should be exposed to regular fire safety drill. Fire-fighting is not an easy exercise. It requires a lot of technical know-how. Fire accidents do not give advance warning, and as such all should be fully prepared for any occurrence. All equipment must be in good functioning order. Loss of artefacts through theft is invariably partial and they could still be recovered but a loss through fire is a total loss. Fire, therefore, is the museum's number one enemy and no effort is too great to prevent it.

Personal safety and security

All museums should feel concerned for the safety and security of their staff and visitors. Efforts should be made to provide reasonable safety and security measures. First-aid kits should be provided to treat minor cases of injury and illness. However, on no account must the first-aider go beyond the duty of providing first aid. All treatments should be referred to a qualified medical practitioner. It is helpful if the museum organises first aid classes where community first-aiders can be trained. It would boost the image of the local museum in the community if it could arrange visits from health visitors and medical officers occasionally.

On special days, every attempt should be made to prevent over-crowding. It is the responsibility of the museum authority to control crowds. Apart from the health hazards which over-crowding presents, damage could be done to displays. The museum should be laid out in such a way that accidents are prevented. Avoid loose railings, wet and slippery floors; the habit of using bottles or other sharp materials on walkways should be avoided. Where safety problems are virtually built into the structure of a monument used as a museum, visitors and personnel should be warned of inherent dangers.

Finally, to ensure adequate visitor safety, certain regulations must be imposed on both the public and the museum's staff. All must be educated to make the museum safe for others.

Conclusion

In dealing with the issue of security in local museums, I have taken into consideration the major factors militating against the provision of a complete package of impossibly sophisticated security, bearing in mind the location of the museum, the available technology, the geographical environment, the limited financial resources, access to and communication with the museum. On the other hand, I have utilised the human factors that could enhance security practice – the cultural web of the community, available human resources, the low crime rate prevailing in

33

a small rural community, the coherent nature of human relations, cultural norms and the communal feeling of belonging and of ownership of the cultural heritage. If these were effectively tapped, the provision of security would be minimal in cost and would be effective enough. However, there must be a concerted effort to generate awareness through education and enlightenment.

Mindful of the factors militating against their use, I have deliberately avoided topics like alarms, automatic gadgets for fire suppression, electronic surveillance equipment like closed-circuit television (CCTV) and the like. I have concentrated more on the provision of physical security based primarily on the human element, which to me is the basis of museum security.

On a final note, I should like to re-echo the fact that the local museum has the singular advantage of being owned by a community that belongs to it, a community that would like its own continuity and prosperity perpetuated. This sentimental aspect of the museum should form the basic of its charter, for it is on that core that the museum should anchor its security.

Notes

Since writing this paper the author died suddenly and tragically while researching museum security in East Africa.

1. May I assume that most of us here, as museum professionals, are aware of the various literature on museum security, especially the big volume prepared by the International Committee on Museum Security and published by ICOM in 1977. It will interest you that although this book has been accepted as a masterpiece eye-opener on museum security, the committee is very much aware of the limitations of its general application and that more work should be done in meeting special needs. The writer, co-operating with another expert, Colonel Robert Burke of the Smithsonian Institution, Washington, D.C., has prepared another book specifically addressed to the needs of developing countries, or developing museums. Everything suggested in the book is virtually practicable in our local museums; however, the limiting factor is funding, since our local museums cannot afford the funds required for effective implementation of the recommendations suggested. It is therefore our duty to reduce our security practice for the museums to the barest affordable minimum.
2. Carl E. Gothe, *So You Want a Good Museum: a guide to the management of small museums*, Washington, D.C., AAM, 1953.
3. *The Conservation of Cultural Property, Museums and Monuments*, XI, Paris, Unesco, 1969.

4 *The Training of Local Museum Staff*

EMMANUEL ARINZE

Local museums, as distinct from national museums, have their immediate community as their focal point in fulfilling the traditional role of museums. By this, they tend to serve the local community first while not shutting their doors to other interests of a national character. It follows therefore that the collections of local museums are a reflection of the local history, the local culture, the local heritage and the local materials of the local community.

Museums generally are an expression of their time, and they represent a tradition that reflects their historical evolution and development. The local museum therefore tells a story that is unique in content and relevance, as its story reflects the history and growth of the community, and highlights the landmarks of the community's evolution. The importance of local museums becomes very apparent when we realise that, because of their uniqueness, they tend to possess an imposing wealth of exhibits of cultural interest, materials of great ethnographic and archaeological value, and they serve as centres of inestimable psychological value to the community.

Stressing the usefulness of local museums, Gerhard Bechthold explained that 'as educational institutions in the service of a genuine humanism, and a means of enabling man to achieve self-awareness independently, to develop his character and find his bearings in a constantly changing and expanding world, the importance of local museums can therefore scarcely be overestimated'.[1] In West Africa the need to establish local museums is being recognised now by various communities. In some countries, like Nigeria, government has given its approval to the various communities, state and local governments

Figure 4.1 Drum of wood, hide and iron, Baga peoples, Guinée
(*Photo: Franko Khoury, NMAfA, Washington DC*)

that wish to establish museums. The 1979 Nigerian federal constitution removed all museums and monuments matters from the Exclusive Federal list to the Concurrent list. This means, in effect, that both the federal, state and local governments and local communities can all now establish and run their own museums.

However, one major problem that stares local museums starkly in the face, more than any other issue, is the problem of finding trained and qualified staff to run them – that is, the problem of training.

The problem

The present situation in most West African museums is that there is an acute shortage of qualified and well-trained personnel to run the museums. This problem becomes much more serious if it is realised that there are no special courses aimed at training personnel to equip them with the expertise required to meet the challenges of such local museums. Museums, be they national or local, are developing today into complex institutions that require high-level expertise and experience, to enable them to keep in step and survive in a fast-changing world. This makes it absolutely essential for museum personnel to train and retrain on a constant basis.

In West Africa, as in other parts of Africa south of the Sahara, local museums are emerging more rapidly than national museums. This can be attributed in part to the economic situation in African countries and also to the low priority given to museums generally in the scheme of things and in the allocation of funds. Consequently, local communities are taking the initiative in ensuring that materials connected with their heritage are not destroyed or abandoned, to their detriment. In the way of this goodwill and the eagerness of communities to establish their own local museums is the problem of non-availability of trained personnel to run and organise them. The problem is acute and calls for urgent action by agencies concerned with the establishment of museums and the training of museum personnel. It is not enough to establish museums without trained staff to run them. It is better for a museum was not to be established than to establish it and hand it over to untrained and unqualified personnel. To do so is to destroy the cultural soul of the nation and the community. It is in this light that training becomes one of the most important and urgent problems facing West African museums today.

By the nature of local museums, and the problems they pose, it is necessary that a specially tailored training programme should be evolved for their personnel. Consequently, in planning this specially tailored programme, we have to be guided by certain basic principles, namely:

1. The educational background of the staff to be trained,
2. The type of local museum the trained staff will work in after training,
3. The period of training,
4. The environment in which the museum is situated.

These basic principles would enable us to plan a viable and positive training programme that would be relevant and useful to the trained staff, the local museum and the community in which the museum is located. Flowing from this is the fact that the training programme for local museum staff should be practical and functional:

1. *Practical*. The training for local museum staff should be practical work-oriented. This will enable the staff to try their hand doing practical things they will be expected to do in their museum. For instance, they should spend more time working in the workshop learning how to assemble and construct showcases, doing colour scheming, lighting and all other activities connected with exhibitions. They should also spend time on objects in the conservatory and doing work in the photographic laboratory – developing and printing films. They should spend time on the actual documentation of objects in the museum store. In this way they will come in direct contact with various objects and develop the ability to document them accurately.

To achieve this element of practicality, classroom work should take not more than 30 per cent of the entire training period while practical work should consume 70 per cent of the entire training period.

2. *Functional*. The training offered should aim at equipping the trained staff with the skills to work successfully in the local museum. Trainees should acquire relevant skills, develop expertise and be exposed to various stimuli that will enable them to be practical functional museum officers at the end of their training. The need for functionality of training becomes apparent when we realise that the museums they may work in may be small, with a very small staff.

This makes it necessary, therefore, that their training should encourage local museum staff to be versatile and adaptable to a variety of situations.

Another dimension in the training of local museum staff is that, at the end of their training, they will be expected to be all-rounders,

37

generalists of museum work and master of all. This in addition to versatility will enable them to wear different hats at different times. They may function as curator, exhibition officer, education officer, as photographer, conservator or administrator.

To be able to produce this type of staff for the local museums, I suggest the following framework for training staff: attachment to a national museum, and formal training in a museum training school.

Attachment to a national museum

In this form of training, the staff will have to work in a national museum as trainees. The purpose of this is to expose trainees to the various aspects of museum work and give a general training that will introduce them to the right museum culture. This method of training would enable the trainee to be directly involved in the actual work of the various sections of the museum, right from the planning stage to the real practical execution stage. It is a functional and practical approach that will stimulate the interest of trainees – arouse their curiosities, sharpen their reflexes and activate their potential. It will give them an overview of what it means to work in a museum.

Further, it would enable the trainee to develop the habit of working with his hands; observe at first hand how the expert works and deal with intricate matters about the museum; ask questions arising from direct observation and activity; acquire experience and expertise in a practical way. It would also enable the trainee to acquire the habit of teaching his colleagues by doing when he returns to his local museum.

To achieve maximum results through this method of training, the training period should be programmed not to exceed a period of six months. However, if the national museum is not a big one, and is without some of the components of a museum, such as a conservation laboratory, photographic laboratory, education services, exhibition service, documentation service, etc., then the period should be reduced to no more than three months. The rationale for the limited period is to ensure that the trainee is actively engaged throughout the period and that boredom leading to restlessness and loss of interest is avoided.

For practical purposes, the programme should be drawn up in such a way that the trainee would spend not more than four weeks in any one section of the museum. In each section the trainee should participate actively in all the programmes and activities of the section. S/he should for purposes of this training be subjected to close and constant supervision by the co-ordinator of the programme and be expected to write a report about their experience at the end of their work in each section. The trainee should be encouraged to participate in all practical work done, including field trips, excursions and archaeological expeditions where this is possible.

Using the national museums in Nigeria as a model for the purpose of analysis, the following sections exist where a trainee can pursue an attachment programme:

1. *Exhibition section.* The trainee would be involved in the planning, construction and execution of exhibitions, in selecting objects, writing labels, constructing showcases and the actual mounting of the exhibition.

2. *Education.* The trainee would participate in all educational programmes of the museum: programming, programme formulation, lectures, guided tours, children's programmes, holiday programmes for schoolchildren, workshops for teachers and various outreach programmes.

Figure 4.2 Carved wooden head with peg to stand in wooden pedestal, Guinée (*Photo: British Museum*)

3. *Audio-visual section.* Trainees would learn at first hand how to use audio-visual equipment and materials.

4. *Archaeology section.* Trainees would actively participate in all archaeological expeditions and learn the simple techniques of excavation and the analysis of artefacts.

5. *Documentation section.* Trainees would be exposed to documentation techniques and shown how to handle objects that come into the museum. They would also learn the various security techniques and materials used in the museum and learn how to organise a museum store.

6. *Ethnography section.* Trainees would be exposed to simple methods of field research and how ethnographic materials can be collected in the field. They would also learn how to analyse the various materials that are collected.

7. *Photographic section.* Here the trainees would be taught simple photographic techniques and how to operate a simple but efficient photographic documentation process in the museum.

8. *Administrative section.* Trainees would learn basic administrative methods that would enable them to organise a local museum effectively with the minimum of staff. In addition they would learn how to organise and run a small library in the museum.

The expectation would be that, with effective planning, and well executed programmes, local museum staff, at the end of the attachment training programme in a national museum, would have taken the first confident step in preparing themselves to work well in a local museum. However, to ensure that such staff had the required theoretical training that would enable them to tackle theoretical issues would require a further training programme. This, however, should be in a museum school possessed of the necessary experts and equipment for such training.

Formal training in a museum school

To make this training meaningful, the trainee should have completed secondary school education or would have attended a teacher training college. The aim of this component of the training programme would be to expose the trainee to the theoretical aspects of museum work. Here trainees would acquire the basic museographical techniques that would enable them to perform well, ensuring proper conservation, restoration and presentation of the museum collections to the public and the local community. The training would enable them to develop and run educational and cultural programmes in the local museum for the benefit of members of the local community.

As it is expected that each trainee would work in a local museum in their community at the end of the training, it is very important for the training centre or school to evolve a special training scheme tailored to meet the needs and aspirations of the museum. Such a programme should, in the words of Philip Ravenhill, be a 'custom-fit' training. Consequently in programming such a scheme, certain issues should be borne in mind:

1. The type of collections in the local museum,
2. The facilities available in the local museum,
3. The educational background of the trainee,
4. The type of community the local museum is situated in.

For the purpose of formal training in a museum training school it is expected that the course should not last more than six months in the first instance. However, an additional three months could be added if it was considered necessary to enable the trainee to combine theory and practice effectively.

So far, in West Africa, there are two museum training centres, based in Jos, Nigeria, and Niamey, Niger Republic. The Jos Centre for Museum Studies was established in 1963 to train museum technicians, although more recently it has expanded in scope to train middle-level personnel in both technical and museum techniques. At certain times, graduate curators and other museum professionals who also have a university degree do train there. The Niamey centre was opened only to train museum technicians. The Niamey course lasts for six months, while the Jos Centre course runs for ten months. In addition, the Jos Centre programme is for English-speaking Africans only, while the Niamey course caters for French-speaking Africans.

However, for the purposes of this chapter, the Jos programme will be used as a model for discussion. The Jos Centre for Museum Studies runs an intensive and extensive course for its students. It combines effectively the concept of theory and practice and ensures that students spend about 60 per cent of their course doing practical work in the laboratory and in the field. The Jos Centre runs the following courses:

1. Museum administration.
2. Museology.
3. Museum documentation.
4. Introduction to ethnography.
5. Museum education practices.
6. Museum exhibition techniques.

41

7. Preservation and conservation of cultural objects.
8. Introduction to the archaeology and history of Africa.
9. Introduction to cultural anthropology.
10. Museum audio-visual techniques.
11. Architectural conservation and the maintenance of historical buildings.
12. Graphics.
13. Museum security.
14. Introduction to ethnomusicology.
15. Introduction to museum library science.
16. Photography.

In addition, all students do a four-week internship in the National Museum, Jos which shares the same grounds with the centre and at the end of the course each student writes a project (long essay) in an area he/she is most interested in. Also, as part of the course, field trips and excursions are organised throughout the period of the course, and all students take part in these field trips and excursions.

It would appear that such a programme as that run by the Jos Centre would be too much for the training of staff who will work in a local museum that is based in a local community. However, the programme can be modified appropriately to meet the particular needs of the local museum. This notwithstanding, it must be borne in mind that the essential ingredients of proper museum training must not be sacrificed so as to make the training offered too shallow to be effective. Perhaps it can be argued that the scope of the programme for the local museum staff should be structured to suit them by ensuring that local dimensions and peculiarities are injected into the course content.

In addition, special programmes can be run both at the Jos and the Niamey centres specifically for the staff of local museums in West Africa based on a scheme drawn up to meet the special needs of local museums in the sub-region. Such courses should be run on an experimental basis in the first instance and later integrated into the normal programmes of both centres.

Some problems. Like national museums, local museums are faced with certain fundamental problems that affect the training of staff. Such problems include:

1. *Lack of funds*. Museums in West Africa are generally not well funded. They are given low priority rating in government policies and in the allocation of funds and resources. The position is even worse in the case of local museums. The community may set up a museum on its own, independent of government aid; however, the local communities

are not always financially buoyant, and so what emerges is that the local museum staff are always painfully small and funds allocated for training are even smaller.

2. *Lack of status*. In West Africa museum workers rate low among other workers. This invariably affects their status. Thus the museum profession does not seem to attract highly qualified people. Worse still, when people are trained they tend to move to more lucrative jobs at the expense of the museum. The local museum staff are already local in rating, and so attracting qualified staff for the local museum calls for extra effort.

3. *Lack of opportunities*. Local museum staff are limited in scope; they need to be trained and retrained to broaden their horizon and so need to be exposed to interaction with colleagues in bigger museums.

4. *Lack of staff*. Not many qualified people will aim to work in local museums. This creates a situation of acute shortage of qualified personnel; it needs special effort to attract suitable staff who can be trained for the local museum. To improve the situation, the museum should be given a character that will enhance the personality acceptance of its staff.

Conclusion

The local museum has a vital role in the future of museums in West Africa. It may serve as a catalyst in the museum movement in the sub-region; it may be the bedrock of the museum service for us in the face of a shortfall in the establishment of nation museums due to the severe economic realities of our day and the low rating museums enjoy in our countries.

Consequently, we must begin now to encourage our local communities to build and nourish local museums; we must prepare and train staff to meet the challenges of the local museum. We must train the local museum staff to develop an intimate knowledge of the local community, its history and its material culture, and to develop the ability to read and discuss family histories of members of the community. Above all, we must train our local museum staff so well that they can ensure the continued existence of our local museums, as such museums may be all that is left when our national museums as we know them today cease to grow and develop.

43

Note   1. Gerhard Bechthold, 'Regional museums', *Museum* XXI, 2 (1968).

Bibliography   Adedeji, Adebayo (ed.), *Problems and Techniques of Administrative Training in America*, Ile-Ife, University of Ife Press (1969).

Bechthold, Gerhard, 'Regional museums: development, function and organisation', *Museum* XXI, 2 (1968).

Fernell, Graeme, 'Central government support for local museums in Scotland', *Museum* XXXV, 2 (1983).

ICOM News 21 (1968)

ICOM, *A World of Museums*, Paris, ICOM, 1983.

Lacouture, Felipe, 'Aspects of staff training', *Museum* XXXIV, 2 (1982) .

Muller, J. C., 'Training centre for museum technicians in Africa, Jos, Nigeria', *Museum* XVIII, 3 (1968).

Pubal, Vaclav, 'Vocational training publications', *Museum* XI, 2 (1958) .

Reilly, Wyn, *Training Administrators for Development*, London, Heinemann, 1979.

5 *Basic Infrastructure Problems in Local Museums*

CLAUDE DANIEL ARDOUIN

As soon as the problem of setting up a museum, whether national or local, is raised the problem of its infrastructure arises too: on what technical basis should the museum operate? There is no intention here of laying down a single type of infrastructure for local museums: social, cultural and economic realities differ greatly from one country to another. Objectives, too, vary. In fact it is impossible, and it may even prove dangerous, to seek to project a single type of infrastructure for local museums. Rather, we shall try and identify a number of key aspects which may assist the thinking of those involved in the creation of local museums.

The question of the basic infrastructure deserves special attention. Whatever the nature of the local museum, whatever the governing body it comes under – government, private, local community – it must meet a number of basic requirements, first for it be viable, and second so that it does not become the graveyard of what it is supposed to protect and promote – the cultural heritage.

The choice of basic infrastructure for local museums is conditioned by a number of fundamental factors.

The country's general economic situation

In countries like ours it is usually very difficult. Whether they are supported by the government or by the community, there is no point in hoping that museums will have significant financial resources. So the museum must be capable of functioning effectively with very limited means. It is always possible to get a museum built and equipped with outside funding. However, when the building of a local museum depends initially on external funding alone there is a serious danger that such funding may run out and not be renewed or replaced by some other source of support. That often happens. In such a case the

45

museum may quite simply gradually go downhill to the point where it ceases to exist.

The existing museum system in the country and relationships between the various museums

This is proving to be of ever-growing importance in the difficult situation our countries are experiencing. The fact is that it is most unlikely that any local museum will be equipped with an adequate infrastructure. It is equally unlikely that, for years to come, there will be all the technical staff required for the operation of a complex infrastructure.

In fact there seems little justification for seeking to equip a local museum to the highest level. In the vast majority of cases the potential so created would hardly be exploited. The importance of the museum system of a country lies in the technical assistance that the various museums – national or local – can offer each other. There are various possibilities, one of which might be to concentrate on building up the infrastructure of one or several central, national or other museums so that they can provide other museums with technical support as and when needed. That does not rule out local museums assisting each other. Whatever the different variants, the key thing is that the overall set-up should function efficiently, hence the importance of a system of museums.

General objectives assigned to local museums

This links up with a wider debate on the general definition both of a museum and of a local museum. Would it be desirable to conceive a local museum as a mere fixed space for exhibitions and contemplation, as is unfortunately the case in many museums, even national ones, today? Should a local museum be made to focus solely on the conservation of its collections, in the most narrowly technical meaning of the term?

If we accept that the local museum should be a cultural and social tool that is an integral part of its environment, then its activities must be envisaged on several levels.

1. *The preservation and protection of the cultural heritage* is one of the objectives of every local museum. This activity must be envisaged on two levels: (a) *internal:* its own collections and borrowed collections; (b) *external:* in the cultural or geographical area covered by the museum, it must help to discover and protect the cultural heritage.

2. *Knowledge of the cultural heritage.* This covers both the collections and the cultural phenomena to which they relate. It is not enough simply to gather and conserve collections; it is also necessary to know them, as well as the cultural phenomena of which they are part.

3. *Dissemination of the cultural heritage.* This covers a wide range of possible activities directed at the public, within as well as outside the museum.

Other objectives can be envisaged, if the development of the museum allows. For example, the museum might act as a scientific research agency.

Technical requirements

It is important to look at these, since the spread of independent moves at community level to promote the creation of museums should be accompanied by concern to avoid museums becoming the graveyard of their *raison d'être*, i.e. the cultural heritage. However, technical requirements should not militate against the flexibility necessary for the smooth running of local museums.

Technical requirements may vary according to the conditions mentioned above. However, all the possible combinations rest on a specific foundation: the museum's collections. The collections are the core from which everything develops. Technical requirements rest on the primacy of the object, the collections – whether they are the museum's own or on loan. The requirements involve knowledge both of the objects and of the means of their preservation or dissemination.

All this suggests the following as minimum technical requirements:

1. The formation of collections, even temporary ones,

2. Their documentation, which is particularly necessary for local museums, because they also have to work with borrowed items. Once returned to their owners or custodians, such items may suffer an unpredictable fate or even disappear, but the museum will still have the information about them.

3. Dissemination, which can take various forms: exhibitions, educational programmes for schoolchildren, programmes aimed at different publics, etc.

Since the basic technical requirements are based on the collections, the museum's basic infrastructure must from the beginning enable it:

1. To hold collections,

2. To keep them in a good state of preservation and security.

3. To deal with problems of their conservation, either within the

47

museum or with the help of another museum or conservation centre,

4. To give the public wide access to the museum and its collections through exhibitions and various outreach activities.

If this initial objective is achieved, a solid base will have been created for the subsequent development, should that prove possible, of the local museum concerned. Of course, the infrastructures will also depend on:

1. The scale and complexity of its activities, which are a function of the social and cultural complexity of the population among whom it is developing, and the extent of its geographical coverage,

2. The nature of the museum and, where relevant, its specialisation.

3. The basic programmes selected, themselves dependent on the general situation, availability of resources, etc.

4. However, if the local museum meets the requirement that its collections should be in the best possible state of conservation and dissemination, a big step will have been taken, which will make it possible to envisage increasingly complex activities. As an example we might take the preliminary studies for a proposed regional museum at Sikasso in Mali.

It was conceived as an average-sized museum serving quite a large area, the region of Sikasso, with a considerable population. As the region has not suffered drought, the general economic conditions are better than in other regions of Mali. In addition, the population had already, without intervention by the State, carried through major infrastructure projects, such as the sports complex at Sikasso. The thinking behind the programming of the basic structures of the museum was based on these general conditions. It was proposed that the museum should be equipped with a number of technical facilities:

1. A space for stock where the museum's collections would be conserved,

2. A space where collection documentation would be carried out and managed,

3. Minimum facilities for photography, making it possible, for reasons of documentation and security, to photograph the museum's collections as well as particularly important items of the cultural heritage in the region. The facilities are very small-scale, with two sets of equipment for taking photographs, one 6x6 and one 35 mm, as well as developing and copying equipment.

4. A small conservation unit where the simplest processing could be undertaken. It was envisaged that complex operations would be carried out with the help of the Musée national in Bamako, whose job it is,

when needed, to provide back-up in conservation, photography and audio-visual activities.

5. The space allocated to the preparation and presentation of exhibitions was decided on after the arrangements for carrying out basic museum activities such as stocking, conserving, documenting and securing collections. In fact the guiding principle was that, whatever the scale of the museum or the size of its staff, these activities constitute the basis on which a viable exhibition programme ought to rest.

6. It was envisaged that the courtyard of the museum would be used for educational activities.

Once this core had been made operational, it would be possible to contemplate extending the museum's activities, especially those aimed at the public.

At first sight, this set-up may seem complex. Yet it should be appreciated that it is intended for a regional museum whose activities involve a large area, and the defined core can be put in place in stages.

In conclusion, there is no typical structure. In each case the factors mentioned above will influence the conception of the museum's infrastructure. Yet, with the growth of demands by communities for the creation of local museums, care must be taken to avoid unstructured development. That is why it is vital that we should make strict demands on ourselves first of all. Such demands will be understood by those calling for local museums if we spell out the reasons behind them.

6 *Regional Museums on Archaeological Sites*

JEAN-BAPTISTE KIETHEGA

At its seventeenth session in November 1984 the General Meeting of Unesco adopted a convention on the protection of the cultural and natural heritage. Burkina Faso ratified that convention at the meeting of the Council of Ministers on Wednesday 15 May 1985. Both internationally and at the State level, these measures reflect awareness of the need to preserve and protect all the elements that go to make up our cultures, and especially those that lie at their very foundation.

The contributions of archaeologists and museologists to the realisation of the objectives set out by Unesco in the area of preserving the heritage can be vast. Archaeologists will have the role of identifying, sometimes of unearthing, always of explaining, the remains of our past. Museologists will have the role of promoting the archaeological discoveries through their own techniques of dissemination and involving the public.

This book thus calls for archaeologists and museologists to work together so that their activities are complementary, rather than continuing to jog along in the sort of isolationism that is still typical of some of our museums or archaeological arrangements in the sub-region. My topic opportunely provides a chance to consider the complementary relationship of archaeologists and museologists. We should try first to grasp the nature of the archaeological sites in our sub-region. By their nature and situation archaeological sites offer unrivalled possibilities of exploitation for museum purposes.

Archaeological sites in West Africa[1]

It would be pretentious to claim that all archaeological sites in West Africa are known. Far from it. In fact, even where they have been started, archaeological inventories are still very incomplete. We need not go into the reasons for the slow progress of archaeological prospecting in our sub-region and indeed the rest of black Africa. Let us simply say that despite its being acknowledged as a priority for our national archaeological teams, the slow progress of the archaeological inventory seriously hampers the drafting of archaeological research plans and programmes at the national level and militates against sub-regional co-operation. What is most deplorable about this situation is that it condemns sites to destruction by man or nature simply because they have not been surveyed; and this failure to survey them means that it is impossible to carry out urgent salvage operations where necessary.

A complete survey of our archaeological heritage thus cannot be compiled today, but we can still attempt a typology of sites already listed. Whether they are prehistoric or historical, their nature, site and situation will be the dominant factors in their use as sites of local museums.

In all our countries there are many prehistoric remains which have been listed and sometimes studied. Usually they are: workshops where stone was cut or polished; megalithic sites; neolithic settlements with an abundance of personal items, tools and clothing; rock carvings, paintings, inscriptions, etc. Such remains are mostly found in the Sahel: Mauritania, Senegal, Niger. They are sometimes located in inaccessible and uninhabited areas. The infatuation of the foreign public with prehistory has led to the systematic looting of the surface material of some of these sites.

Prehistoric sites

Figure 6.1 Wooden bowl with figure, Bissagos Is., Guinea-Bissau (*Photo: British Museum*)

51

Island sites   In the last few years research has been conducted in a number of countries on sites whose chronological dates differ but which have in common the fact that they are isolated by lagoons (the Eotile islands in Côte d'Ivoire[2]) or shifts in water courses (Ayourou, Firgun and Yamm-Gungu islands in Niger[3] and three islands in the mouth of the Saloum and Senegal rivers[4]).

These island sites may correspond to a particular civilisation, like the Eotile in Côte d'Ivoire, or may have acquired importance because an historical figure stayed there, for example the island of Askia Mohammed Touré.

Anthropomorphic mounds   Anthropomorphic mounds are assuredly the archaeological remains that are most frequently encountered. These are the sites of old villages, abandoned for whatever political, economic or sociological reasons. Wars of conquest or civil wars, the constraints of an itinerant slash-and-burn agriculture or the ravages of endemic diseases have sometimes, in the more or less distant past, forced peoples to migrate, leaving behind them ruins that have shrunk as the years have passed. Today, these mounds are found scattered over the bush, and sometimes unexpectedly in the middle of the forest,[5] their surface littered with fragments of all types of pottery.

These mounds may be close to existing villages, but they are not spectacular and do not attract tourists. Their wealth lies in the material that is hidden underground. Hence looters engage in unauthorised digs in the search for treasure. These sites, the most common of all, are also the most difficult to list, precisely because there are so many of them, but also because they do not immediately attract attention. They can thus be looted with impunity, especially as they are easily accessible.

Citadels built on heights   By citadels we mean all buildings designed for defensive purposes. Perched on the plateaux and outcrops that are typical of the region, they are difficult of access. These defensive structures were in fact built on the heights because of their advantages for observation and the difficulty of access.

In Burkina fine illustrations of this type of archaeological provided by the site of Diamon, 30 km north of Aribinda, a town situated in the north of the country. We also have the example of the Tankamba shelters on the Gbanangou 'cliff' in the south-east of the country near the Benin border. In Niger my colleague Gado Boubé has also located some, including the site of Shatt, in the Azaoua, in the north of the country.[6] Citadels built on heights are to be classed among the most picturesque sites in West African archaeology.

Rock shelters

These may be natural caves half-way up the slopes of hilly ground. Where the caves are man-made, as dwelling places and for defensive purposes, the entrance is usually hidden from outsiders. The only tell-tale signs are that the soil is more or less compacted or there may be low internal walls of dry stones or earth.

There are few personal items visible without excavation. The only visible objects are granaries, either made of clay or in holes dug in the ground. In Burkina we may mention the examples of the cave at Borodougou and the Peridan site, both near Bobo Dioulasso. These caves vary in size; at Borodougou the main cave is 100 m².[7]

In this category of site may be included the numerous caves carved out of the cliffs at Bandiagara in Mali, which have been the subject of archaeological study for some years by a team from the Institute of Anthropology of the State University of Utrecht in the Netherlands. This team, led by R. Bedaux, has already yielded an abundant harvest of information and materials.[8] The caves contain the remains of a cultural unit, that of the Tellem, the first occupants of the Bandiagara 'cliffs', with 100–300 m bluffs; these sites are among those most visited today by tourists from all over the world.

Fortified walls

Fortified walls offer the public the most spectacular ruins. Built of stone or sun-dried brick, they are monumental achievements that compel admiration for the creative genius of the builders of the past. Principal among them are the remains of the defensive systems of the kingdoms and empires that followed one another in West Africa: protective walls, warrior *tatas*, fortified palaces.

Examples are the walls of Sikasso in Mali,[9] the fortified enclosures and *soukala* dating from the Zaberma occupation in Gurunsi in Burkina[10] and the remains of the palace at Abomey in Benin and that of Naba Kango at Ouhaigouya in Yatenga in Burkina. To this category of ruins also belong large-scale but as yet enigmatic buildings such as the ruins of Lobi where the borders of Burkina, Côte d'Ivoire and Ghana meet, whose origins are still debated by historians and archaeologists.[11] Paradoxically, these fortified enclosures are the sites which most urgently require intervention to salvage them from the destructive

53

workings of nature, as well from the human beings who are in the habit using them for building materials.

Relics of economic activity

No one is unaware of the role gold played in the Sudan in the medieval West African economy, mainly in the trans-Saharan trade. There are still numerous archaeological remains of this mineral's production between 9° and 15° west and 2° and 16° north.

Gold-producing provinces were famous in the past – Bambuk, Bure, Baoule, Ashanti, Lobi. today some of the mines have been rediscovered and industrial exploitation is going on alongside forms of traditional working in which activity varies from year to year and place to place, and which sometimes makes use of the waste left by ancient workers. The gold-bearing places were generally exploited by superficial scouring, open trenches or shafts linked to one another by galleries without props. The old gold production sites thus offer a landscape littered with mounds of waste and pitted with thousands of shafts that have since fallen in.[12]

The old gold production sites are thus ones where the ore was extracted in lateritic placers. In addition, iron production sites provide ironworkings that are in some cases very extensive and smelting furnaces that are sometimes still well preserved. These sites are usually to be found close to existing villages, the siting being dictated by the presence of ore and the means to exploit it (water to pan it, water and trees to build furnaces and make the charcoal needed for smelting). The local creative spirit developed such varied techniques for smelting iron ore that the morphology of relics varies from region to region.[13]

One could end the list of types of archaeological sites here. This typology takes no account of chronology. It is far from exhaustive overall. It does not, for example, include other categories of site such as the religious monuments of animism and Islam, which may be difficult to include under any of the above headings. Similarly, monumental sites such as Koumbi Saleh, Awdaghust, etc., should be classified separately.

As can be seen, although some of these archaeological sites are situated in modern capital cities, where the national museums are, most of them are scattered in the provinces, in desert, bush or forest or in villages. That cultural objects should be left in their environment is a position that no longer has to be defended. Now therefore we must turn to the question of how to preserve these cultural heritages through regional museums.

At the Valbonne symposium in France in May–June 1978 French-speaking archaeologists from sub-Saharan Africa and Madagascar had the opportunity to take stock of how well our archaeological and historical heritage is being conserved. The meeting listed the chief agents of destruction of our heritage. They are:

1. Climate,
2. The use of the land for agriculture,
3. Bush fires,
4. Large-scale development projects,
5. Traffickers of all sorts,
6. Tourists and co-operators.

The meeting also debated the purpose of our future regional museums.[14]

Archaeologists are unanimous in recognising that as a general proposition museums highlight the object, be it archaeological or otherwise. But museums as we know them in Africa extract the object from the network of relationships that it maintains with the geological, ecological, spatial and cultural context.

There is no need to spell out that for the archaeologist what counts is the information that the object can provide, thanks precisely to the network of relations that it maintains with its context. Consequently the archaeological object ought not be isolated from its environment, or else it is likely to provide no information. In addition to the fact that the object cannot truly provide information when it is removed from its cultural context, any removal of the object may precipitate disastrous consequences at the scientific level for itself and for the other evidence of the past to which it belonged. An object displayed in a museum or anywhere else acquires a commercial value that it did not previously have. It thus enters the commercial circuit and attracts the attention of collectors, antique dealers and traffickers of all sorts to deposits of similar objects. Even when conducted very methodically, archaeological excavation already involves destruction of the site. Exhibition of the material excavated and publications that show the location of the remains are other dangers for sites that have not yet been excavated and enjoy little protection. Should they be left unexcavated, as some advocate? We think not, and similarly we feel that, despite the danger that museums themselves pose, they should not be suppressed but be more organised, so that they meet the need for the dissemination of knowledge about our past through its material remains and about the

Archaeological sites and regional museums

What sort of regional museums on archaeological sites?

55

need to preserve sites and conserve cultural property.

To that end, and without going into museum techniques with which we are quite unfamiliar, we feel that the archaeological material yielded by excavations must, after laboratory analysis and study, be restored to its cultural context, even if the present inhabitants of the site have nothing to do with the people who produced the civilisation exhumed.

It is moreover rare that there is no link at all between the past and present populations. However, the migrations that have been a feature of some peoples in the sub-region must be taken into account. Whatever its size, the regional museum will have to be a structure that makes it possible to meet the following requirements:

1. To protect cultural objects from the unwelcome attentions of unscrupulous individuals and from the natural agents of destruction. The last point is especially important for the monuments excavated by archaeology, since excavation leads to a new process of erosion. In order to protect the object or monument archaeologists can make their contribution by including preservation of the remains in their research programmes. They must, however, work closely with museum specialists so as to use the most appropriate conservation techniques.

2. To protect sites in the locality by keeping an eye on them and making the population aware of the need to conserve cultural property. Archaeologists and museum experts could carry out urgent salvage operations on sites already excavated or currently being excavated or areas likely to contain archaeological sites.[15]

3. To bring out the importance of objects and monuments. To do so using traditional museum techniques will not be enough. Thought will have to be given to how museums can become integrated into the cultural life of our communities, and not remain as a canker on it. One approach would be to have local people responsible for local museums. Indeed, that is the sole hope for the true protection of our cultural heritage. But it is quite useless to regionalise museums as one decentralises a government department if conditions are not studied so that local museums have a real impact on the people. To get that involvement of the local population going, why not associate youth associations and other cultural organisations with the activity of increasing popular awareness?

What archaeological sites for local museums?

It must first of all be noted that, in a given locality, several types of archaeological sites may coexist. The problem is to choose the most suitable one as a local museum. We are not suggesting here that the local museum should specialise according to the nature of the existing site(s). But sites do not yield material in identical quantities and of an identical quality. The one that meets a number of conditions – such as the scale of the remains, geographical position or ease of lay-out – will be preferred to another one that is cramped or inaccessible. Naturally the possibility of choice can exist only in cases where a locality has several archaeological sites. The choice of archaeological site will also have to take account of its cultural content, pride of place going to sites that have a direct relation with the culture of the existing population.

Local museums definitely cannot be created on every archaeological site without raising enormous problems of conservation infrastructure, as well as human problems. The fact is that local people taking over local museums does not completely eliminate the need to train museum technicians. Choices will have to be made bearing all these considerations in mind, taking cultural areas as the fundamental basis.

Among the types of sites listed above, some may be recommended as the basis for a local museum:

1. The sites of ancient capital cities or major cities, such as Koumbi-Saleh, Awdaghust, Kong, Begho, Niani, etc. offer the greatest advantages as homes for local museums.

2. Fortified enclosures also have the advantage of including structures which, once they have been restored, might be home to a local museum. This is particularly true of *soukala* and some warrior *tatas*.

Figure 6.2 Entrance of fort which now serves as the historical museum. Gorée, Senegal (*Photo: Christraud Geary, National Museum of African Art, Washington, DC*)

57

3. Rock shelters might also act as exhibition halls, with new arrangements for access and exhibitions. When they contain rock carvings, paintings or inscriptions the local museum will have to be housed separately. Unfortunately this type of site has rather limited usable areas.

4. Island sites sometimes have the advantage of being picturesque but above all they offer security, and security is facilitated by the position of the site.

5. Mining archaeology is little developed in the sub-region. However, in some countries the current state of discoveries makes it possible to set up technological museums on the actual production sites. These technological museums could be dynamic museums contributing to the rehabilitation of some craft production. Such rehabilitation of the technological heritage is indeed called for by some countries in the sub-region that are members of WAEC.[16]

The other types of site (surface prehistoric sites and anthropomorphic mounds) offer no particular criteria for selection. To summarise, despite the slowness of archaeological excavation and the low level of investigations of known sites, our region has numerous archaeological sites which may serve as bases for regional museums. But the objectives of regional museums need to be settled first, as well as the way in which they are to be integrated into the local culture. This volume is itself one step, giving an impetus to the history of West African museums: archaeologists and museum specialists are thinking about new types of museums and the complementarity of archaeological and museum-related activities. Installation experts should also be summoned to this task.

Notes

1. The sole overview of archaeology in West Africa is already over a quarter of a century old: R. Mauny, *Tableau géographique de l'Ouest africain au Moyen-Age,* Dakar, IFAN, 1966.

2. Our colleague Jean Polet has been conducting research on these islands for several years.

3. Gado Boubé, *Tradition orale et archéologique: introduction à la connaissance des sites archéologiques de la vallée du Moyen-Niger,* Niamey, University of Niamey, IRSH, 1977, p. 9.

4. Cyr Deschamps and G. Thilmans. 'Nouveaux tumulus Coquilliers découverts dans les îles de Saloum (Sénégal)', paper presented to the second conference of the West African Archaeological Association, Bamako, 1978.

5. Jean Polet 'Fouilles d'enceintes à la Séguié', paper presented to the Bondoukou seminar, 1974.

6. Gado Boubé, 'Notes introductives sur les sites de la vallée du Moyen-Niger et les statuettes en terre cuites de Karegooru', Niamey, University of Niamey, IRSH, 1977, p. 3.

7. J. Henninger, 'Signification des gravures rupestres d'une grotte de Borodougou – Haute-Volta' *Notes africaines* 64 (1954), p. 106.

8. R. Bedaux, 'Tellem, reconnaissance archéologique d'une culture de l'Ouest africain au Moyen-âge: les appuie-nuques', *Journal de la Société des africanistes* XLIV, 1 (1994), pp. 7–42.

9. R. Bedaux, 'Rapport intérimaire sur les fouilles dans le Delta intérieur du Niger (Mali)', Institute of Anthropology, University of Utrecht.

10. In June 1985 a master's thesis on these Gurunsi ruins was defended by Yago Ousmane at the University of Ouagadougou.

11. Numerous studies by M. Delafosse (1917), E. Ruelle (1905), J. Bertho (1952), A. Labouret (1920) and R. Mauny (1957) have not lifted the veil of mystery surrounding the Lobi ruins. It is still not known who the builders were or when they were built.

12. J. B. Kiethega, *L'Or de la Volta Noire*, Paris, Karthala, 1983.

13. A seminar on the 'History of iron metallurgy from the mine to the metal before the adoption of the indirect method' brought together scholars from Africa, Europe and Madagascar in Paris in March 1983. The papers presented show the variety of techniques.

14. CNRS, *Les Recherches archéologiques dans les Etats d'Afrique du Sud, du Sahara et à Madagascar*, Valbonne, 1978, pp. 151–2.

15. J. Tixier, 'Archéologie de sauvetage en Afrique', paper presented to the symposium on archaeological research in the states of sub-Saharan Africa and Madagascar, Valbonne, 1978, pp. 151-2.

16. The seminar organized by Unesco and WAEC in Ouagadougou in March 1982 on setting priorities in the area of scientific research made such a recommendation.

7 The Legal Framework of Independent Museums

PAPE TOUMANI NDIAYE

The secretary of the Smithsonian Institution, S. Dillion Ripley, said on the occasion of the bicentenary of the birth of the founder of that honourable institution that if it were to have a motto other than the sibylline phrase 'for the increase and diffusion of knowledge among men', it should be 'for the quest for what is not fashionable, using means that are not usual'. The present volume might appropriate that phrase, since it invites us to reflect, through the 'legal framework of independent museums' on what 'is not fashionable'. It must certainly be agreed that independent museums are not in vogue in our countries. Which makes 'not usual' the 'means' of providing them with a legal framework.

That is why I crave your indulgence for the gaps and limits inherent in the treatment of a topic which is outside the ordinary, since the person who is dealing with it is not, strictly speaking, a museum specialist. I intervene, not to edify you on a subject that I have mastered, but in the hope of awakening some interest, provoking some thought and calling forth opposition.

Problematic of independent museums

An independent museum is an institution conceived and managed by a community or a foundation, endowed with legal and corporate personality, managing its own financial resources and organising its services in a structure distinct from that of the State, run by individuals directly appointed by the people or foundation concerned. Independent museums so defined do not occupy a very prominent place in our various States. Hence any approach aiming at the creation of a museum institution meeting this definition must first tackle the multiple problems whose solution is the key to the proper functioning of the museum and guarantees its independence.

60

In the first place, there is the crucial problem of viability. That means, above all, cultural viability assessed in terms of the qualitative results achieved in conserving and disseminating the local cultural heritage, the renewal of artistic creation and the contribution of the museum to the national development effort.

The viability in question is not measured solely by the number of tourists attracted and the number of works or tickets sold. In any event, the promoters of an independent museum have to assess the effectiveness of their institution by questionnaire surveys aimed at the public. In the light of the responses obtained, the museum's *modus operandi* will be modified in the direction desired by the population whose satisfaction, in the final analysis, legitimises the institution's existence. Realism requires us to stress that the financial viability of the museum is a condition of survival, since the community cannot permanently provide it with the necessary resources. In other words, an independent museum is under an obligation to resort to the most suitable means to ensure for itself fixed revenues to enable it to meet recurrent expenses.

But, if I may be allowed the expression, for a museum to find money is a work of art. It is up to the management committee and the director to identify and exploit sources of finance, showing a concern for proper open and democratic management. A number of conventional ways of mobilising funds may be cited briefly:

1. Subscriptions from members of the association that manages the the museum,

2. Receipts by the museum,

3. Grants from the State, municipality, non-governmental and international organisations,

4. Fund-raising activities: dances, fights, lotteries etc.,

5. Income from a craft or agricultural activity attached to the museum,

6. Sponsorship, etc.

You will already have guessed that we are here putting our finger on an essential aspect of the functioning of museums, public relations. They consist in making the environment aware of the problems of the museum, being willing to inform the various publics and helping them to get to know and understand the institution and inspire their sympathy and confidence. They undoubtedly constitute a strategic concern of the museum's communications policy.

Grafted on to the touchy question of viability are other obstacles of a formidable complexity that can easily hamper the proper functioning of the museum or result in the loss of its independence. Among them are blockages consequent upon the political, economic and social structure of the society, such as:

1. Economic underdevelopment, which constitutes a negative factor because it permanently engages the knowledge, resources and energies of the people in so-called 'development' activities. And, without these means, an independent museum taken over by the community is doomed to failure.

2. Social underdevelopment, which is also a negative factor given the illiteracy that it engenders and the importance of ethnic behaviour, which are all so many centrifugal forces.

3. The political underdevelopment of a population habituated to passivity towards an authoritarian administration is similarly a brake on the museum's independence.

Other aspects of social relations negatively condition a self-managed museum, notably:

1. The multiplicity of languages, which hinders the circulation of ideas and dissipates effort in a series of translations,

2. The denial of differences. On this, systematic study of the image of the Other should be instituted in all museums all over the world, given its political, religious and philosophical implications,

3. Violations of human rights.

4. Political and military conflicts.

5. Massive emigration, which leads to chronic depopulation.

6. Uncontrolled tourism, leading to the looting and degradation of cultural property.

Alongside these negative features, which are syndromes of male development, may coexist other positive ones such as:

1. The spirit of initiative and enterprise,

2. Social and cultural associations,

3. Artistic and cultural groupings,

4. Tolerance of and a taste for differences,

5. The practice of hospitality,

6. Cultural tourism, etc.

Observation of the African environment suggests that the unfavourable factors constitute real grounds for the promoters of an independent museum to have second thoughts. However, they can be overcome by the determination of a community to gather its strength to fight against fatalism and take its fate in its own hands by breaking with long-established habits whose burden of inertia militates against any attempt at social transformation. Every society, even the most deprived, retains intact within it latent forces of rebirth for a better life.

It is up to the promoters of an independent museum to identify the potential and organise it in an adequate legal framework.

The legal framework of independent museums

To return to the problem posed, it is easy to observe that in Africa the vast majority of museums are totally dependent on some public agency, be it the State or a municipality.

This situation derives from characteristics common to the Third World, where the State, although financially constrained, has to look after all social/cultural institutions, with or without the support of the national or international community. This paradox is a good illustration of the precarious situation of museums in countries whose priorities are the struggle against desertification, famine and illiteracy. It brings out starkly the problematic of all museums in Africa in general, and local museums in particular, the latter being served only after the all-powerful and budget-devouring national museums. It has become clear to everyone concerned with museums in Africa that it is a matter not simply of creating museums on any of a multitude of grounds but of making them function, and function well. In many respects the State is no longer enough. Moreover, what are our States enough for, now that they are prey to financial difficulties deriving from maldevelopment and world economic crises? If that is so, then the question arises urgently of how to create a museum and ensure its subsequent functioning outside the State sphere.

We feel that the alternative is involving the people in this creation by ensuring them a role that is not limited to contributing funds, materials or objects to exhibit. On the contrary, their responsibility must be preponderant in every phase of the process of setting up such an institution, from its conception to its everyday management. Simply mentioning this alternative should be enough to show that we are abjuring the conventional approach to take a stand that challenges bureaucratic systems in which the needs of the community are always expressed by the administrative authorities.

It is glaringly obvious that there exists a trend favourable to the establishment of independent local museums, but we are indeed obliged to recognise that it has still hardly touched the population at large, so much does the whole notion of a museum, in most of our societies, continue to be a matter for the elite. That is one reason why there must be an appeal to creative workers and intellectuals who, faced with this alternative, might be tempted to take refuge in research inspired solely by their own discourse, without involvement in social movements, which is where we take our stand. Thus to stand aside would be extremely harmful and would inexorably lead to the creation of a museum for the elite and for tourists.

If it is possible to act, the first thing that must be done is to embark on a whole programme of enhancing awareness that will eventually make it possible to observe among the population at large signs that are sufficiently compelling of public demand for a museum. Once the general interest in the project is established, then organisation of community participation can begin within an adequate legal framework. To do this, the promoters of independent museums will need to form themselves into a legal association and set up within it a management committee responsible for running the museum, by resort to the legal provisions that guarantee freedom of association. To this end there are several forms of association.

First there is an ordinary association which needs no statement of objectives to function, and has no legal personality.

At another level is a form of partnership, which can have a legal basis and capacity authorising it to proceed at law, acquire title to the ownership of property, manage the contributions of its members and administer the association's own premises as well as the buildings necessary for achieving the goals it has set itself. The statement of intent of the partnership is made to the administrative authority of the locality where the partnership has its headquarters. The promoters of the partnership will have to specify its name, its purpose and its head office, as well as the names and occupations of those who, in whatever role, are responsible for managing it. A receipt will be issued for this statement. Theoretically, in the following months, the statement should be made public and inserted in the official gazette. It is only from the date of such publications that the partnership will acquire corporate personality. This is the status that accords with a 'friends of the museum' association whose role is limited to educational work and collecting funds or objects.

A partnership that wants to manage a museum must be recognised to be of public interest by decree or administrative order, depending on the legislation in force, upon a report by the Ministry responsible for internal affairs after receiving the opinion of the department concerned, in this case the Ministry responsible for culture. This type of association comes under the same code of obligations as a partnership but it may in addition receive gifts which, above a certain value, require the approval of the Ministry of the Interior.

A partnership recognised to be of public interest responsible for the management of an independent museum can receive gifts and subsidies under certain conditions; e.g. that it will:

1. Present its registers and accounting records whenever the Ministry responsible for the Interior or the prefecture so requests,

2. Present to the local authority an annual report on its financial situation.

In addition, the law places such a partnership under an obligation to provide in its rules that any member of the community may belong to it without distinction of age, sex, race, religious, political or philosophical adherence, of whatever socio-professional category, on the basis of respect for secularism. Furthermore, it must be expressly provided that all views and beliefs, save those contrary to the International Declaration of Human Rights, can be expressed within it. The rules and regulations must by law specify the mode of recruitment, the criteria of eligibility and the voting method as well as how the partnership's property will be managed and controlled. The standing orders must spell out in detail the statutory provisions,which are always couched in general terms. In short, a public interest partnership is the legal instrument through which the promoters of an independent museum can break the umbilical cord with the State in favour of self-management. But if the major concern of self-managed museums continues to be conserving and developing the local cultural heritage, a twin reality weighs on them: recourse to the government in order to work within a legal framework, and the determination to be independent of the State. In other words, given that relations between an independent museum and the authorities are necessary, they should be clearly spelled out so that peaceable and fruitful relations may develop between them.

Relations between independent museums and the State

To our mind, relations between an independent museum and the State are founded on the principle of the contribution the self-managed museum makes to the cultural decentralisation policy that our States are pursuing with varying results. Decentralisation assumes the freeing of initiatives at the base, in a direction favourable to the spirit of responsibility and enterprise. It includes the exercise by individuals of prerogatives of the government. It is a democratic demand. It is true that in some countries it takes courage to try to create an autonomous museum when the State alone is empowered to manage a public institution, of whatever nature. In such a situation, while avoiding confrontation with the authorities, an independent museum comes to stand as a demand for freedom of expression.

Again, the danger lies in pressure from political parties for whom any community grouping is a means of manipulation and agitation. To be and remain independent the museum must beware of two reefs which, like Scylla and Charybdis, will threaten it throughout its existence: depending on the State for everything and trying to do without the State altogether. It must draw its strength from legal recognition by the State and its autonomy *vis-à-vis* the government. Often institutions that do not depend on the government strongly dislike local authorities meddling in their business affairs in the name of a fierce sense of self-management.

But in our countries no museum is in a position to do without the State, from which, as we have already seen, it seeks legal recognition, possibly the enjoyment of a piece of land on an appropriate site and, above all, technical assistance from the national museum. In return, an independent museum acknowledges the right of oversight, freely granted, by the national museum over its methods of conservation, protection and restoration, in the interest of the collections. This technical advice and support role includes watching over standards of security and document processing. Within the limits of its capacity, the national museum is looked to for training and upgrading. The two institutions must work out a network of communication and co-operation with a view to exchanging experience, equipment and exhibitions. Without prejudicing its own options, it is desirable for the approach of the independent museum to fall within the global mission assigned to the country's museums. This is what makes a protocol governing the multiple links between the two entities essential as they make a complementary but never conflicting contribution to the same cultural policy. To return to the relations between an independent museum and the State, the former may benefit from the assignment to it of civil servants whom it would be beyond the resources of the museum's treasury to take on.

The State too, under some legislation, has the right to concern itself with respect for the rules and the management of a public interest partnership that is authorised to receive gifts and grants from the national and international community. This makes it necessary, even useful, for the partnership to accept the obligation on it to admit oversight by the State for the stricter management of property that is deemed to belong to the community. In our opinion, this right of oversight cannot alienate the autonomy of the partnership and the management that it has freely given itself. The mistake to be avoided is to reject intervention by the authorities as long as possible and then turn to them when the harm has already been done. The State can then act only as ambulance man or fireman and not as a moral and legal authority. Institutionalisation of the right to oversight by the State must be freely agreed to by the partnership as a sign of its commitment to open and honest management. However, such oversight should be limited to the right to supervise the books and ensure respect for the regulations and standing orders. Any other prerogative would tend to hamper the museum's autonomy.

We must not omit to stress that the public interest partnership managing a museum is neither a trade union nor a political organisation. The State is therefore required to see that its apolitical character is respected. For all these reasons, relations between an independent museum and the State must be clarified from the very beginning, so that there can be guarantees that help towards the establishment of reasonable relations based on mutual respect for the rights and obligations of the two parties.

As regards the case of Senegal, which we know best, we feel that the legal situation of such a partnership, as defined in article 821 of Law 68-08 of 26 March 1968, enables it to carry on its activities with the greatest independence provided it is willing to apply the rules of democracy. The Senegalese constitution, which recognises the separation of powers, along with the clear and precise definition given of the notion of tutelage by the State, lead one to be optimistic.

Conclusion

An independent museum is a rare institution in Africa. As an option it is becoming more and more widespread, as a manifestation of determination on the part of a community to undertake 'with its perishable hands' the building of a lasting monument. It is a challenge to itself and to passivity in the area of culture. It is not a challenge to the State; on the contrary, it is a contribution to the development process. It is a utopia, a dream whose realisation will not be without setbacks which will have the effect of reinforcing determination.

8 *Plea for a Traditional Arts & Crafts Museum*

ALEXIS B. A. ADANDE

Figure 8.1 Baga mask, Guinée
(*Photo: British Museum*)

Kan xoxonu wɛ yé non gbin kan y y do
(Fon version of a proverb widely known in the Ajatado world: 'It is from the old cord that you weave the new one …')

Conservation of the cultural heritage and economic development are concepts which may at first appear contradictory, or even quite incompatible, but each summarises succinctly the urgent problems facing the peoples of black Africa today: to find a way of safeguarding the core of the ancient cultural heritage without, in so doing, sacrificing the improvement of the living conditions of the whole population.

In fact it is only when they are approached as separate, quite unrelated domains that culture and heritage, on the one hand, and economic and social development, on the other, can appear opposed. With the convergent development of contemporary museology and the broadening of the meaning of the term 'development' to include quality of life, it is now possible to go beyond the apparent contradiction of the two concepts. And that is something that is all the more urgent because the bulk of research work in the human sciences in black Africa, especially in cultural anthropology and archaeology, points to the rapid deterioration of the cultural heritage – both oral and material – under the combined effects of social upheavals that affect traditional structures, on the one hand, and, on the other, the erosion of the 'archives in the ground'[1] by man and nature. The obliteration of the cultural heritage is aggravated by the break that schooling, among other things, continues to maintain between those who preserve traditional knowledge and traditions, on the one hand, and the young educated, on the other.

In this general context, every scholar concerned about the safeguarding of a centuries-old heritage understands that, especially when his investigations touch material culture, they have meaning only if

Figure 8.2 Headdress of wood, abrus seeds, fibre and resin, Koro peoples, Nigeria (*Photo: Jeffrey Ploskonka, Gift of Milton and Frieda Rosenthal, NMAfA, Washington, DC*)

they are accompanied by the collection, study and public presentation of the samples collected and of the techniques by which artefacts[2] were made are described and can be recovered and reproduced. But the fact is that the principal parties concerned with the salvaging of this knowledge are the communities within which they arose and developed or were maintained, with varying success, down to the present day. Better still is that, when some of these old techniques have been updated, they can meet present-day needs, as would appear to be demonstrated by positive experiences of auto-centred community development. In the light of the above remarks, a museum of material culture – in this case an arts and crafts museum – looks like one of the ideal instruments to back up an active policy of endogenous development. As such, the museum will be set up at the local or regional level close to the basic community.

Figure 8.3 Carved wooden stool with four supporting figures, Bambara , Mali
(*Photo: British Museum*)

Figures 8.4a, b, c Creating a traditional pot (*Photo: Adande*)

According to ICOM typology a traditional arts and crafts museum can be classified in the category of specialised museums: 'a specialized museum is a museum whose research and displays are devoted to a single topic envisaged in its various aspects, whether these relate to the fine arts, archaeology, history, natural history, ethnography and folklore, science and technology, the social sciences, trade and communications, agriculture, etc.; the geographical scope of these programmes may be limited to a single clearly defined region or extend to the international arena. The basis of their programme is commonly one of the dominant features – whether a phenomenon or an activity – of the region where they are established'.[3] Note that this general definition suggests that a traditional arts and crafts museum gives pride of place in its programme to a topic related to the dominant activity of the everyday life of the area in which it is situated at a particular point in history, or which still is.

To spell out the definition of an arts and crafts museum – a definition that takes on board the contributions of active museology[4] we shall conceive it as a complex of built spaces and open areas housing collections of technical objects, evidence of the old traditions of knowledge and local innovations, along with activities associated with training and transmitting the ancestral knowledge to the younger generation and adults who would otherwise remain ignorant of it. The museum will thus constitute what can only be described as a conservatory – in the broadest possible meaning of the word: a school for demonstrating and teaching ancient artisanal arts and crafts.

For the traditional arts and crafts museum as defined above, the following will be the main objectives:

1. Those assigned by ICOM to any museum, i.e. 'to present collections of cultural property for the purposes of conservation, study, education and pleasure',[5]

2. In addition to these research, conservation, education and cultural action functions there will be a more dynamic dimension deriving from a more global conception which embraces the social and economic role it has to play through recovery, dissemination and creation.[6]

Let us go through the objectives to be assigned to this type of museum one by one.

These involve making the museum an institution which will contribute to resolving the essential problem of the transmission of ancient technological knowledge, from its last holders to the next generation.[7] As they are currently conceived, neither schools nor colleges nor even technical institutions are in a position to take on this task. At this level we touch on the difficult and complex question of the relationship between schools and universities and the cultural heritage in general, and the technical heritage in particular, in the countries of black Africa. The issue is complex because it raises many others, including that of social psychology, or even psychopathology. Otherwise how else can we interpret the total rejection of the values of the ancient civilisation and technology, especially among those who have been to school, the intellectuals of the 'modern African elite'?

Alexis B.A. Adande

This knowledge was of course deemed outdated, and thus unworthy of any but ethnographic interest, during the colonial period, and the share of responsibility that lies with colonial ideology for these negative attitudes on the part of 'educated' Africans towards their own cultural heritage has already been demonstrated elsewhere.[8] Yet it is disturbing to observe how little the numerous reforms of educational systems undertaken since the independence of African States have succeeded in filling this breach.

It will thus be the task of the museum to promote a *rapprochement* between traditional technicians and young people who would otherwise be kept in ignorance of learning and knowledge that are the fruit of a long and rich tradition of practical experience. The museum will also be the place where adults who so desire can come and learn, where necessary, to fill the gaps in their own knowledge of the common heritage.

Scientific objectives

While rehabilitating traditional knowledge, the museum will act as a framework for research at several levels of teaching, fundamental research and applied research.

Educational research. Scientific study of traditional arts and crafts can be a good way of introducing schoolchildren to technology, by enabling them to discover in a concrete way a number of laws of physics, chemistry, human biology, etc. This educational action which stresses the heuristic value, for young people, of enquiries outside the school walls[9] can and must also have as feedback the cultural enrichment of traditional technicians, to whom might be revealed in

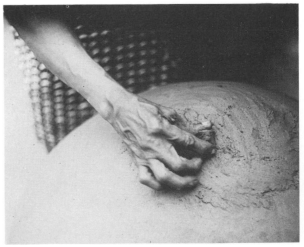

the course of the exchanges, some general laws that guide some of their gestures or some of their technical choices.

Thus the gap between traditional technology and industrial technology can be seen as no more than a difference of degree in the mastery of means. If this objective is attained, it will help to reduce the inferiority complex that black Africans feel towards industrial technology, reconcile them with local technology and develop in them once again the spirit of creativity.

Fundamental research. Traditional arts and crafts are also worth studying for themselves, as products of the human spirit, of African man, placed in given ecological contexts. From this angle, technical procedures must be minutely studied, reconstructed if need be and conserved just like finished products. But craft products of often remarkable quality do not reveal the simple, even rudimentary, tools that were used to make them; in this connection one might mention the instruments of the potter and the beauty of the dishes that emerge from her hands.[10] It is the gesture, the movement of the hand that is essential in these crafts, which are truly arts, transmitted from one generation to the next.

The gap in craft traditions makes it urgent to record on film or some other medium the manual skill of the artisan, which, in these conditions, is as, if not more, important than the tool which served to make the technical object or material culture.

Applied research. Scientific study of traditional arts and crafts must also lead to the formation of a data bank of the various technical solutions by the different peoples studied, according to their own cultural traditions and the problems with which they were or still are

Figure 8.5 a, b, c,
Demonstrating the art of
the traditional potter
(*Photo: Adande*)

73

Figure 8.6 Decorating a
traditional pot (*Photo: Adande*)

confronted. In fact the advantage of the establishment of museums of
this sort evenly over a given territory is to facilitate and bring forward
the study and safeguarding of a heritage that is today in a precarious
situation because it is threatened with oblivion.

The scientific data thus collected will make it possible to have
available to the communities concerned and researchers a body of
technical knowledge which might serve as a basis for the development
of improved technologies that are immediately adaptable to improve
living conditions. This practical aspect of applied research should help
to raise the scientific awareness of the district where the museum is
established and prepare the more dynamic individuals in the community which manages the institution to take on board new, more
efficient techniques, so as to be in a position to choose the best options
among those that come from outside and promote innovation.

To sum up, museum-related scientific research requires the con-
currence of several disciplines, including the history of the natural
sciences and health, not to mention the resources of teaching. The
multidisciplinary approach is essential to guarantee that collections are
put together scientifically and that a representative corpus of traditional
arts and crafts is assembled.

Cultural and social objectives   The interest in ancient knowledge will in all certainty develop a greater
awareness of the need to safeguard the cultural heritage. The develop-
ment of such a movement can only enrich the cultural life of the
community and promote openness to other cultures, near or far.

Similarly, better understanding of manual crafts cannot fail to enhance the social standing of such activities. This latter aspect is important because in contemporary black Africa technicians in general and artisans in particular tend to be looked down on. This anachronistic attitude is inherited, in some societies, from an old caste spirit and was surely reinforced and developed during the colonial period by systematic depreciation of traditional arts and crafts and, by extension, of everything to do with manual and technical work.

It is true that today there has been a marked shift in attitudes towards technology but this trend needs to be accelerated and consolidated by the impetus that would be made possible by the existence of a traditional arts and crafts museum, which would both open minds to creativity and innovation and put down roots in the ancestral cultural heritage.

These objectives ought no longer to be regarded as subsidiary to museology: to the extent that the museum is integrated into the social fabric, it is no longer outside the essential concerns of the community it serves. In this sense the museum has a public relations role to play between artisans and visitors:

1. By rehabilitating artisan crafts and their products, the museum, through its educational activity, can help to modify the consumption habits of visitors and get them to opt for local products, often of better quality than some shoddy manufactured goods which may even in some cases be positively harmful to health or the environment (for example, plastic containers of unstable chemical composition used to hold food or drinking water; non-biodegrable products that pollute our towns and countryside, etc.). That is the museum's indirect economic action: altering consumption models and changing the scale of values in the direction of a better quality of life, through a more rational exploitation of local resources and less dependence on the outside world. At the level of a single country it will help in reducing outflows of foreign exchange and redressing the balance of payments.

2. More directly, the products made in the museum's workshops can be put on sale, with a quality label and a guarantee of authenticity, when needed. The museum operates as a shop window at this level and its catalogues ensure the dissemination of publicity for its products. At the national level the establishment of local arts and crafts museums facilitates effective planning of craft production.

To the extent that other chapters have already looked at the technical and organisational aspects of the local museum and its relations with the administration and the central museum structures, I shall not linger on these points but will recall some principles that I see as useful to a local traditional arts and crafts museum.

In the first place, we must consider the principle of community management as a prerequisite, with financial autonomy; the community must also have wide freedom in the fundamental choices of the museum's programme, with the central administration giving its scientific support and technical help.

The museum will thus be organised around the central theme which will have been decided on in the light of the activities that were or are typical of the district in question: textiles (fabrication and processing), basketry, pottery, metal-working, traditional architecture, stock-raising, fishing, agriculture, ways of storing and processing food products, culinary arts, local pharmacopeia, etc.

As an institution managed by the community to serve as an instrument of its own cultural, social and economic progress, the museum must be in harmony with the local architectural heritage. However, so far as possible, the museum will be allocated the most space possible, with a view to its future extension.

Naturally, in line with its architectural traditions, the community will be both the owner and the project manager of the museum. Nevertheless, for obvious reasons of efficiency and to put to good use the achievements of contemporary museology alongside ancient practical knowledge, it is recommended that technicians from the central museum and historical monuments services should be closely involved in the development of the museum's programme. Similarly, technicians must be attentive to local practices in conserving objects and be capable of putting them to use for building up reserves and displaying items to the public. In this connection it would be desirable for the permanent technicians of the local museum to be recruited within the base community, and that suitable training should be given them, either in the framework of the national museum or in the museum structures of an African country better equipped in this area.

The collections will be stored and displayed in one or several pavilions, around which will be set up demonstration or teaching workshops in a park planted with typical local flora. Alongside the display areas, there will be a space set aside for documentation (library, audio-visual, etc.) which will serve also as a research site for any who want to deepen their knowledge.

However, the proper operation of a museum of whatever size presupposes the resolution of delicate problems of management on several levels: administrative, financial, scientific, conservation and maintenance techniques, acquisition, documentation and dissemination of information.

That is why it is vital that the experience of creating a local museum should be carried through with care and that the initiative should be largely left to the qualified representatives of the community, so that the project enjoys the necessary understanding and facilities from the administration. For the community it will be the chance to exercise in practical terms the self-management of its cultural heritage.

Influence and co-operation

As is normal, the main priority of the local traditional arts and crafts museum will be to meet the needs of the community within which and for which it operates. Its influence will be ensured by the participation of members of that community in its activities and cultural programmes, especially schoolchildren and teachers. In addition, periodical publication of leaflets and items in the local press will ensure that people know about the museum. On this level, the use of national or vernacular languages along with the official language will ensure that the newly literate know what is going on and will also consolidate and enrich the technical and scientific vocabulary of our languages.

Finally, the local museum will seek to develop its relations with other local museums inside the country and abroad. Thus arrangements for the exchange of collections and documents will have to be set up in order to ensure that this special arena of communication that a museum is now called upon to be active in is truly open to the world.

The authorities responsible for culture in our countries should, as local museums are set up, encourage the establishment of a network of co-operation between these basic institutions and encourage or instigate the establishment of regional museums as structures to consolidate the museum movement. In this same perspective, it is not inappropriate to recall the necessity for inter-African co-operation in scientific research in order to stimulate the circulation of information (research programmes, results of surveys and fieldwork, etc.) and – why not? – to encourage joint study teams. Thus a databank could be built up quickly and more cheaply which would be available not only to professional researchers but also to local museums in West Africa.

In any event, it would seem to be essential that in the very near

Alexis B.A. Adande

future there should come into being at the national or inter-African level an arts and crafts museum or conservatory bringing together both information about the ancestral technical heritage and information about contemporary technology adapted to the social/cultural conditions and needs of peoples to show the contribution of each area of civilisation to the known technological heritage of humanity. For, to take up the apt formula of Smita J. Baxi, curator of the Crafts Museum in New Delhi, the traditional arts and crafts museum must become 'a reference centre at the service of artisans and a centre of cultural exchange for all'.[11]

Summary The problem of conserving the cultural heritage in black Africa is all the more crucial because this part of the continent is going through a period of historic transition and rapid transformation which faces oral societies with the threat that whole swathes of their ancestral heritage will disappear for ever. The seriousness of the situation does not escape the peoples affected, nor researchers concerned with the preservation of knowledge that is often many centuries old; efforts are sometimes made, not without success, to record some aspects of the pre-colonial cultures. However, traditional craft techniques and trades appear to be irremediably condemned in the face of the massive transfer of industrial technologies and above all under the avalanche of imported manufactured goods.

In order that the treasure which pre-industrial African arts and crafts represent may be preserved from oblivion and placed at the service of cultural, economic and social development, it is suggested, at least as a first step, that museums should be set up that might play the role of true conservatories of traditional technologies and as places for the dissemination of practical knowledge capable of being adapted to present day needs or of constituting a foundation for future innovations.

Notes 1. 'Archives in the ground' is an expression which describes all material objects on or under the ground that are evidence of the activities of people who lived in a given area.
2. A term to describe all products due to the activities of man: tools, buildings, works of art, etc.

78

3. Definition adopted at the meeting of the ICOM Committee on Specialist Museums, Yugoslavia, September 1960. Seminar organised by ICOM on 'Les problèmes des musées dans les pays en voie de développement rapide: travaux et documents muséographiques', Neuchâtel, 17–25 June 1962, p. 89.

4. MNES Info, 'Déclaration de Québec', adopted by the first Atelier International Ecomusées/Nouvelle Muséologie, *Bulletin de formation* 4 (March 1985), p. 6.

5. ICOM seminar,. 'Les problèmes des musées dans les pays en voie de développement rapide', Neuchâtel, 17-25 June 1962, p. 28.

6. Smita J. Baxi, 'The craft museum at New Delhi', *Museum* XXXI, 2 (1968), pp. 97–9.

7. Alexandre S. Adande,'L'impérieuse nécessité des musées africains', in *L'Art nègre*, Paris, Présence Africaine, 1951, second edition 1966, pp. 163, 165.

8. Abdoulaye S. Diop, 'Musée et développement culturel et scientifique', *Bulletin de l'Institut fondamental de l'Afrique noire*, 38, sér. B, 2 (1979), pp. 354–8.

9. Alexis Adande, 'Un exemple de recherche archéologique: enquête réalisée par les élèves de l'école publique de Bensékou', *Recherche pédagogie et culture* 55 (1981), p. 82.

10. Alexis Adande and Goudjinou Metinhouse, *Potières et poterie de Sè: une enquête historique et technologique dans les Mono béninois*, Université national du Bénin, 1984, pp. 18–22.

11. 'The craft museum at New Delhi', p. 102.

80

9 The Local Museum at Pobe Mengao · Burkina Faso

MEDA SANHOUR

This museum was a great 'first' in Burkina Faso. It was in 1979 that the people of Pobe Mengao – particularly the young people – carried through the project of a house museum with the aim of safeguarding, conserving and displaying what remains of the artistic, archaeological and artisanal riches of Lorum. Having seen the ravages among the old artistic and touristic traditions of the whole region of the far north of Burkina Faso – at present in the province of Soum (capital, Djibo), the Kurumfe (or Kurumba) people have decided to build a local museum to house a few objects that testify to the traditional culture of Lorum.

Backed by a French archaeologist, Bertrand Gérard, the museum became a reality in 1979 on the basis of very slender means. The building, wholly of mud, is 7.25 m long and 3.5 m wide, with three openings – a door and two windows. All the internal surfaces of the walls have been rendered in mud and the floor is of pounded earth. To display the objects, a raised earth ledge has been built along the walls.

Bertrand Gérard supplied all the roofing for the museum, and the people supplied the labour. Thus Pobe Mengao's ambition was soon realised, at the same time throwing down a challenge to the Burkinabe authorities and museum professionals.

The museum's collections include pottery, ceramic ware, farming implements, weapons, head-dresses, staffs, figurines, masks and leather work, 132 objects in all, and sixty-eight ceramic tiles. They come from all over the province of Soum, where Pobe Mengao is situated, and some neighbouring localities, such as Ouahigouya (in Yatenga) and Kongoussi (in Bam).

The people acquired all these objects by simply picking them up where they lay (pottery), by purchase and by gift. The important thing for the people of Pobe Mengao was to possess a locale outside their homes where they could gather together and make available to the

Figure 9.1 Wooden mask of cow, Burkina Faso (*Photo: British Museum*)

public objects testifying to their history and their culture. It is a striking achievement in a region which is one of the most disadvantaged by nature in our country (Sahel).

By creating this museum the people proved their determination to restore and uphold their region through its culture. Although the scientific methods of museology are not all applied in the museum, its existence *in situ* is concrete evidence of the determination of the people of Lorum to stand up and be counted in the area of culture.

From the time the idea of the museum was launched to the actual completion of the building, no officials of the department responsible for culture, and for museums in particular, had been informed of it. Only four years later, because of the deterioration of the building, were officials of the Musée national approached with a request for cement to repair the building. After that a joint mission was organised with the university to go and take note of the existence of the museum.

In our view, the museum exists, since there is a building and collections. There are staff, but they are not fully qualified, they are too few in number and they are not permanent. They consist essentially of young volunteers who look after visits and clean up after working in the fields during the day. The collections have no identity tags. For lack

Pohe Mengao, Burkina Faso

Figure 9.2 Wooden dance headress, Burkina Faso (*Photo: British Museum*)

of permanent staff, the museum is not open regularly. Given all these handicaps, some connoisseurs and professionals may doubt whether it really is a museum. But is a museum a museum only if it is built according to Western or European ideas? In the African context, what conditions have to be fulfilled for there to be a museum? In the case of local museums is it essential to meet all the conditions laid down by 'professionals' if we are to speak of a museum? In the specific case with which we are dealing, should we reject or suppress this museum because it does not meet the standards we set? Can or must a local museum meet the same requirements as other national or regional museums in the West or elsewhere? Those are some of the questions raised for me by the existence of the museum at Pobe Mengao.

Everything should be done to sustain and improve this museum, which, after all, expresses the determination of the people who set it up according to their means and their environment. If significant alterations are made to it – with or without their consent – will the museum still be theirs?

At present the museum has its drawbacks, notably the lack of trained staff. To remedy that, the officials of the Musée national are proposing to offer technical help by providing a number of volunteers with some basic training, and also to discuss with those responsible for the museum and the locality improvements that might make it possible for the museum to meet the challenge. Intervention by the Musée national and decision-makers at the regional level is absolutely vital if this local museum, the only one of its kind in Burkina Faso, is to survive and attain its objectives.

Meanwhile, the local museum at Pobe Mengao has been ticking over since its creation. It is closed more often than not, and is not well known among the public; to learn of its existence one has to go to the region or enquire at the Cultural Heritage Directorate in Ouagadougou or of people at the university. It thus needs everybody's help, professionals or not, to take off and achieve its aims.

10 *Socio-historical factors for Improved Integration of Local Museums Zaranou & Bonoua • Côte d'Ivoire*

ADOU KOFFI

The purpose of this chapter is to present two museums in Côte d'Ivoire, set up following local initiatives. It involves in fact two quite different experiences in terms of both their origins and the way they are managed. Analysis reveals, however, that their creation follows general principles that could be used for new experiments. The museums at Zaranou and Bonoua are remarkable in that they are perfectly integrated into their environments, whence the title of the chapter. But, to appreciate their originality better, they must be put in the context of Côte d'Ivoire's previous experience in this area.

In Côte d'Ivoire, and perhaps elsewhere in Africa too, the tradition of museums that goes back to the colonial period cannot easily be continued because of the fact that the collections were often acquired without the participation of nationals and the sole criteria that governed their selection were aesthetic delight and ethnographic curiosity. Precious information was overlooked, making much of the collections unusable. Furthermore, the newly independent States that have resolved to continue the museum tradition, far from overcoming the shortcomings of the institution, have been chiefly concerned to make it a prop of national prestige.

The consequence of this attitude is that grandiose museums have been built, but the most basic provisions for their proper functioning have been neglected. Often, even staff training does not follow. Thus a museum, even a specialised one, will open its doors when the country has not a single technician trained in that area. A final pitfall is the lack of flexibility in the way state museums are run; usually they are integrated into a paralysing administrative structure. In short, Ivorian museums are traditionally marked by:

Difficulties associated with traditional museums

87

1. Lack of integration into the community where they are situated,
2. Inflexibility in the way they are run,
3. Insufficient control of collections acquired under colonisation.

It is in the light of these factors that we may assess the museums at Zaranou and Bonoua.

Two case-studies of Local Museums

The creation of the museum at Zaranou

Zaranou is a village with an indigenous Anyi population of 2,500–3,000 inhabitants in eastern Côte d'Ivoire, 42 km from Abengourou. In 1965, in the framework of a national programme to modernise the habitat, the old village was demolished. This operation was a significant event and made it possible to judge how devoted the rural population were to their traditional way of life, which was seriously affected by it.

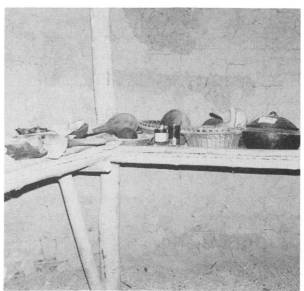

Figure 10.1 (left). Agricultural implements (*Photo: Koffi*)

Figure 10.2 (below) Detail of exhibition (*Photo: Koffi*)

These rural people soon saw behind the operation a determination on the part of the authorities to alter profoundly their communal way of life and launch them into a different experience. They therefore embarked on a timid resistance by staying put until the bulldozers arrived. In the rush, many possessions regarded as of no importance were abandoned in the ruins and it is these possessions and utensils that were carefully gathered up to form the starting point of the museum.

Bonoua is a town of 22,000 inhabitants 60 km east of Abidjan, with an Abouré indigenous population. The creation of the museum followed a political experience that had repercussions in every region of the country. In 1980 Ivorian political institutions underwent a major alteration. For the first time more than one candidate was allowed to stand for elective political offices. The unexpected character of this decision and the lack of prior preparation of the population plunged the country into fierce divisions and oppositions. In numerous localities, under the aegis of the government, recourse was had to grandiose and/or moving reconciliations, but they often failed, with barely suppressed grievances soon reasserting themselves even more strongly than before.

Bonoua, which was raised to the rank of a commune at that time, experienced this situation. And it was to eliminate the fall-out from the elections that the leaders of the region lighted upon the novel solution

*The creation of
the museum at Bonoua*

Figure 10.3 General view of the museum at Parc Mploussoue (*Photo: Koffi*)

Figure 10.4 The open-air theatre at Parc Mploussoue (*Photo: Koffi*)

of creating something that would effectively win the support of the whole population, instead of 'show' reconciliations. An admirable site was selected for the creation of the Parc Mploussoue, a cultural complex including, *inter alia*, an open-air theatre and a museum, which is the centrepiece. It must be stressed that the origin of this project lay in the conviction of its promoters that people recognise themselves through the evidence of the past, despite possible misunderstandings.

Figure 10.5 The bar at Parc Mploussoue (*Photo: Koffi*)

Figure 10.6 Part of the exhibition: a chief and his entourage (*Photo: Koffi*)

If circumstances made the creation of the two museums theoretically possible, their actual realisation benefited from a number of not insignificant advantages.

Particular advantages

Zaranou

The presence in 1964 of a historian and anthropologist preparing her doctoral thesis on the Indenié region, where Zaranou is situated, combined with the existence of an empty building that had originally been intended as an Information Hall, were key factors in creating the museum in that locality. The interest of the historian (Mme Claude Hélène Perrot) in the items of everyday life abandoned in the ruins led her to have them collected together. Subsequently, in an initial stage, the population, well informed of the project, made gifts in the Information Hall building. At the same time, approaches to the administrative authorities led to the provision of exhibition equipment and agreement to pay the person in charge of the establishment. In 1980 the exhibition was moved to a historic building, the former residence of of the French explorer Binger, restored by the Ministry of Cultural Affairs. Today the 15-room Zaranou museum continues to receive gifts from a population who are truly proud of their museum, which they never miss an occasion to visit.

Figure 10.7 Donations to Zaranou museum, including a figure in female dress. (*Photo: Koffi*)

Figure 10.8 Everyday utensils abandoned in the ruins. (*Photo: Koffi*).

Bonoua At Bonoua there was no infrastructure comparable to that at Zaranou. The major advantage here was the fact that traditional society was organised into village age groups; it was in that framework that one of them put up the buildings intended to house the museum. The overall plan of the complex, with four house museums built in the traditional style, was the work of an architect who was originally from the region. Voluntary labour was donated by some age groups. After the completion of the buildings the objects for the collections were given by the population as gifts or on deposit.

In *Bulletin de liaison et d'information de l'Arebo* 4 of the Association pour le développement de la région de Bonoua (May 1982) it is stated: 'these house museums each bear the name of an age group … the

Figure 10.9 Two of the house museums at Bonoua. (*Photo: Koffi*)

Figure 10.10 Local
pottery on display
(*Photo: Koffi*)

choice of the name of each house is not a matter of chance, since the content of each house ... reflects the role that fell to each age group in Abouré society in war-time as in peacetime ...'. Here, even more than at Zaranou, the name of Parc Mploussoue is on everyone's lips; people identify with it and on their days off go there as if on a pilgrimage to see the photo of this grandparent or that old dignitary of the region.

Figure 10.11 The Tchagba house
museum (*Photo: Koffi*)

Figure 10.12 Age-group stools
(*Photo: Koffi*)

Conclusion

Figure 10.13 Part of the
exhibition of photographs
of local dignitaries at Bonoua
(*Photo: Koffi*)

What conclusions can be drawn from these two experiences? We can see that the usual problems which arise in the case of old-style museums, with their rigid administrative structure like 'foreign bodies' have been resolved. The active participation of the population in the establishment of these two museums might be explained by their creation after major events in the history of the communities. Here we find total justification of the words of M. Alpha Oumar Konare in his report to the ICOM meeting in Paris in June 1982 on the planning of museums: 'it is not possible to plan a museum without making contact with the people, especially in developing countries'. It may be added that, in order to guarantee complete success, seeking the help of the population in planning a museum ought to occur at a crucial moment in the history of the community concerned: it is at such moments that its members are most receptive to the idea of such projects, which make their appeal more to their sense of patriotism than to anything else.

11 Proposed Centre of Popular Arts & Traditions Embracing the Local Museum at Boundiali • Côte d'Ivoire

TIOHONA MOUSSA DIARRASSOUBA

Boundiali, the chief town of the department of the same name, situated in the heart of Senoufo country, is 731 km from Abidjan. The department is bordered on the north by Tingréla, on the south by Séguéla, to the east by Korhogo and on the west by Odienné.

The department of Boundiali possesses a seventeenth-century mosque and a number of archaeological sites, together with a large number of centres of traditional art producing a great variety of objects. Safeguarding this rich cultural heritage requires the population to become aware of its scientific value and the short or long-term risks of disappearance that it runs because of the flourishing trade in art objects in the north.

For that reason, and in the framework of a project for a Centre d'Arts et de Traditions Populaires (CATP, Centre for Popular Arts and Traditions) a mission financed by the mayor of Boundiali travelled among the Senoufo and Mande populations of some twenty villages in the department. The mission included a 'museum' side. Two aspects of this mission will be examined in this chapter:

1. Sounding out the population (consciousness-raising) and inventory of the cultural heritage of families.
2. Project design.

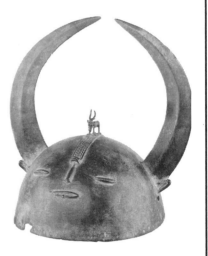

Figure 11.1 Senoufo headdress of cast copper alloy, Côte d'Ivoire (*Photo: Jim Young, NMAfA, Washington, DC*)

Sounding out the Population

Consciousness-raising

It should first be made clear that this was not an opinion survey but simply involved raising the population's awareness of its cultural heritage. For reasons that are peculiar to them, some communities did not respond to the questionnaires that had been drawn up with the survey in mind before the mission actually went out. Given the

95

delicacy with which such a mission had to be conducted, use of this procedure had to be abandoned, as the people were somewhat suspicious of it. Despite the change, the mission achieved its main objective, which was to get the communities concerned to understand that the project in question had a positive impact on both the cultural and the socio-economic development of the region. As a result, if the CATP were to be built, they would be the first to benefit from its numerous advantages, among which two were particularly emphasized.

Inventory After the soundings, the CATP and the safeguarding of the cultural heritage, it was important to get an idea of what might constitute the future collections of the local museum at Boundiali. The inventory of the cultural heritage of a region is not limited to objects that might be part of a local museum collection, but embraces everything, including archaeological sites, historical monuments and traditions. This first mission was limited to the material culture (art objects) for the reasons mentioned above – among others, the disappearance of pieces of value of Senoufo traditional art.

The period chosen (the months of February and March), in the middle of the dry season, was propitious for such a mission. It made it possible to meet a large number of families on the spot and have in-depth discussions with them. After several sessions, that the message had been heard was shown by the influx of different types of objects, including statuettes, bracelets and rings, ankle bracelets, etc., household utensils, firearms, other weapons, chairs of heads of family, heads representing objects of regalia or souvenirs of dead ancestors. These objects can be classified into six categories:

1. Carved objects:

(a) anthropomorphic or zoomorphic objects: statuettes, masks, farming trophies, staffs, *ngoron* horses.

(b) Objects decorated with anthropomorphic or zoomorphic motifs: carved doors, chairs and tabourets, beds.

(c) Musical instruments: ceremonial drums, horns.

(d) Household utensils: plates, spoons.

2. Bronze objects: bracelets, rings, ankle bracelets.

3. Clothing: war tunics, *ngoron* masks, *nayôgi* masks.

4. Weapons: spears and arrows, trade guns.

5. Farming implements: adzes, scythes, scrapers, hoes.

Crafts The department of Boundiali includes quite a number of artisans unevenly distributed over the territory.

Pottery. This takes up very little space, because of women's preference for imported plates and dishes. Pottery is an activity exclusively reserved to women. The few potters located work only sporadically, because of ever-falling demand.

Basketry. This has also been hit by competition from manufactured products. Baskets used to be essential to the housewife but are today being gradually replaced by aluminium basins and bowls. Only winnowing baskets and chicken coops still sell well, as demand for them in the villages remains constant.

Iron-working. Like woodworking, it remains a specialist activity. Like the carver, the Senoufo blacksmith belongs to a social group governed by its own organisation and activity is transmitted from father to son. Unlike other activities, ironworking is quite widespread in the region. At Kouto, at Boundiali, and in other villages, blacksmiths live in special areas. Farming implements (hoes) are their main product. They also make kitchen utensils (ladles, creamers, tripods, stoves) and some ritual objects (bracelets, rings, symbolic animals and statuettes).

Project design

The construction of a museum requires preliminary studies to ensure that it meets certain standards so as to fulfil the mission assigned to it.

The mission

The mission of a local museum like the one at Boundiali is first and foremost to be the expression of the community; it is important to envisage a number of structures before and after construction of the museum buildings. That requires calling upon all available local resources. The formulation of specific objectives is a key requirement on which the effectiveness with which the museum fulfils its mission depends.

A number of environmental factors may favour the development of the museum, or conversely, harm it.

1. The positive features of the society and culture include the associations that are the voice of the community, the wise men or councils of elders, friends of the museum associations, youth associations and artisans' or artists' associations.

2. Negative factors include the dispersed and widely scattered nature of settlements (which prevents contact between the museum and its users), the over-abundance of data (which makes documentation and research work difficult) and the impoverishment of the surrounding community.

97

Planning   Planning is vitally necessary and presupposes on the part of the promoters a degree of aptitude for research and for collecting items and conserving the buildings designed to house them. The local museum being, by definition, a centre for the collection, conservation and dissemination of a given cultural heritage, there needs to be agreement on planning to achieve a number of aims:

Collection and conservation of items. This must be entrusted to specialists, since an object must not be collected simply for its aesthetic value but also for its scientific value (avoiding the empiricism of amateurs). Items to be collected may be made of different materials and have different functions (ethnographic, archaeological or historical objects or natural history objects). Preserving the heritage means preventing it from dying and disappearing forever. It means not only conserving this heritage but above all making it known to the general public and specialist, e.g. by preparing cards to identify and document the objects conserved.

On the levels of dissemination and education all these activities should aim at the following objectives: to enrich the cultural heritage, make it better known, provide visitors with a synthesis of history, promote creativity and expression and offer leisure activities to the wider public.

Building. The museum, being a cultural centre, must be constructed to meet not only criteria as to its siting but also particular architectural requirements. As regards organisation, it must be in harmony with the rest of the local habitat: outside appearance, spatial organisation, layout of galleries, reception rooms, etc.

Management. Initially, the museum must be able to function with at most two qualified staff. The responsibilities of the curator must be more like those of a publicist and a manager and should include:

1. Running the institution,
2. Assessing efficiency,
3. Financing (own receipts, gifts),
4. Managing programmes and activities (exhibitions, social events, etc.),
5. Supervising administrative management,
6. Relations between the museum and the governing body.

Conclusion   This mission provided an opportunity to discover a great variety of works of art and craft products of undoubted scientific interest. Exploitation of the data gathered in the field is continuing. Without wishing to anticipate the conclusions of this basic work, we can already say that the construction of the centre for popular arts and traditions at Boundiali would be welcome in a region where the cultural heritage is rich and varied, where traditions, despite external influences, remain very much alive and where modernity does not mean loss of identity.

12 *A Museum for the Lagoon Peoples of Eotile Country • South-East Côte d'Ivoire*

JEAN POLET

Rather than dealing at length with the practical, technical and financial aspects of the creation of the Musée des cultures lagunaires I shall endeavour, using my experience in Eotile country to understand and analyse the reasons that lead a people to call for the creation of a museum and to look at all the issues that it raises. To do so requires a little regional history.

Eotile country is in the extreme south-east of the Ivorian lagoon network, near the border with Ghana. The islands on the south side of the Aby lagoon were occupied before the arrival of the Portuguese and the Dutch by the Eotile people,whose economy was based on fishing in the lagoon. Written sources are very clear on that point.

At the beginning of the eighteenth century, following upheavals associated with the emergence of the Asante empire, the Anyi occupied the region, defeated the Eotile militarily, drove them out of their islands and deported them to the north of the lagoon. Only a small settlement called Ngaloa survived. All other settlements were abandoned.

Only a century and a half later did the Eotile, after almost losing their language, secure permission to reoccupy the south of the lagoon but, instead of returning to their old homes, they settled all round the water. The islands became sacred sites where ceremonies were held periodically.

These islands are also rich lands and they became sought after, with the entry of the Côte d'Ivoire into the plantation economy, during the twentieth century. But there are very few Eotile and they were the defeated. They did not grow wealthy in the trading economy and they lacked a powerful politician in their midst. After nearly losing their language they now risked losing the land which they saw as their place of origin, and, in fact, in the 1960s and 1970s their neighbours began to develop plantations there.

*A museum for
the Lagoon peoples
of Eotile country,
Côte d'Ivoire*

It was then that the Eotile, seeking to defend themselves, invented a novel strategy. In 1970 the Eotile RDA (African Democratic Rally) committee asked the Ivorian State to designate the islands as historic sites. All the village chiefs claiming to belong to the Eotile ethnic group put their thumbprint or their signature to this request. And, in a decree published in 1974, the islands were designated as the Parc national des Iles Eotilé (Eotile Islands National Park) for 'the protection and conservation of an archaeological site, for reasons of scientific and educational interest, and for the benefit, advantage and recreation of the public'. The management of the park is entrusted to the Ministry of National Education.

That, then, is the official and legal situation. Let us now see the same reality, but differently, taking up the thread of history as I saw it gradually through my work as an archaeologist in the region.

Mid-nineteenth century. The Eotile return to the region after nearly losing their language. They escape direct rule by the Anyi but are now under French rule. whose first establishments in the Côte d'Ivoire were set up in this region, and at the same time.

Early twentieth century. Acculturation proceeds ever faster, with its forms of resistance. The best known is the rapid dissemination of the Harris religion, which leads large numbers of people living along the Ivorian coast to burn their religious objects or statues or throw them into the lagoon. This happens during the First World War.

After the war the role of Ngaloa, that last little village where people still spoke Eotile, becomes important. To resist these manifold attacks from the new world, and so as not to lose out, the elders decide to make one of their own number the receptacle and repository of their culture and above all, of their language. It was with this man that I worked, who was thus the 'mouth of the Eotile'.

When I arrived in Côte d'Ivoire in 1973, just as the work of designation was going on, the Institut d'histoire, d'arts et d'archéologie africains of the University of Abidjan asked me to undertake the archaeological study of the Eotile sites.[1] What, then, were the Eotile asking for?

It was simple fundamental quest for their identity and acknowledgement of what they assert to be their historic rights. And their strategy for achieving it was wholly consistent:

1. To save the language. And that was simple, clear and true: when a people lose their language they lose their culture.

2. To defend themselves against the most obvious attacks from the outside world: encroachment on what they claimed as their territory. This was achieved through the designation of the islands.

3. Using history to prove their rights although they had been defeated. They knew, from oral tradition, how old their contacts were with the outside world and how old was the knowledge written down in what are now called archives. They therefore facilitate historical research by opening up to historians without any difficulty.

They knew how far back their presence went but, since memory no longer suffices in this world, in order to prove it, they turned to 'the white man's methods', to archaeology. All that explains not only the ease with which the preliminary archaeological survey was carried out – sites had already been located, by the population themselves – but also the possibility of unhampered excavation in cemeteries and sacred sites. And as early as 1973 they asked me – and here at last we reach the purpose of this chapter – that all this work should lead to the building of a museum dedicated to their culture, based not only on archaeological finds but also on objects that they had already collected together in order to entrust them, one day, to that museum.

Such are the raw facts that are necessary to understand why a people with a certain historical experience should come to ask for the building of a museum. But setting them out is of interest only for the questions that they raise, that I ask myself and have not resolved. For these questions, in my view, can be asked of most local and regional museums that are not museums devoted to a technology. I shall ask five questions, and offer no answers.

1. To appeal to a historian or an archaeologist is to appeal to a man who reasons in time, who seeks to tease out the course of events, who practises comparison.

But the material culture brought to light by an archaeologist is not enclosed in the concept of 'ethnic group'. If the way of life and patterns of production and consumption of two neighbouring ethnic groups are similar, it is very likely that the archaeological remains of these cultures will not differ very greatly from one another. Whatever their nature, trans-ethnic phenomena are neglected in the African or European historiographical tradition in favour of the differences.

2. Most 'images' of the ethnic group refer to an imagined pre-colonial past – as if society was then frozen. The Eotile, who experienced their first colonisation at the beginning of the eighteenth century, are seeking, against enormous difficulties – which is why they turned to archaeologists – to rediscover this image, which they think to be that of the true Eotile. The earliest things they can remember, the oldest objects in their possession, become by definition Eotile. Naturally, that is wrong, as this example shows:

For the museum of which they dream the Eotile have collected gold weights known throughout the oral literature of the Akan world. These are certainly Anyi but are in possession of the Eotile for precise economic reasons: they were left in pawn when an Anyi became indebted to an Eotile. From the viewpoint of a historian, these objects are part of a system of exchange and their presence among the Eotile is an important sign. As such they are part of the historical heritage of the Eotile. But an art historian who was looking for something ethnic would be led into error.

From the angle that concerns us here, this story shows both the interest and the limits of collection of objects made by a people themselves. A people tends to identify foreign contributions as their own or reject and discount the actual cultural phenomena that they experience every day.

3. After all these years spent excavating the past and living the present of Eotile society it is quite clear that discourse about the ethnic group is not a true reflection of everyday reality. The quest for an ideal past is more and more out of step with everyday experience. I can give an example here too:

About 1925 guinea-worm was ravaging the population of Ettuossika, a village in the west of the Aby lagoon. The disease was eradicated by bringing in a Baule cult from a region some 300 km distant from the village. That cult is still practised each year, sixty years later, but without masks, since they had been rejected by Harrism ten years before. However, the cult is still not considered part of Eotile culture, although it 'mobilises' the village and its riches for several days every year. That leads to the fourth consideration.

4. All the local museums analysed in their local or regional context that we are dealing with here are in fact 'mirror museums', which reflect not the actually existing society, which is difficult to grasp and define because it is undergoing rapid change, but the image that it wishes to project of itself and wants to perpetuate. They are never instruments of communication between different peoples. They are not in the least tools of communication or means of knowledge of the Other.

But – naively, no doubt – I have always found pleasure in learning of different worlds by visiting museums, even if I was also looking for the specificity of man there too.

5. The last question is doubtless the most serious. There is always talk of the necessary 'political will' for the creation of local museums. But that political will is always taken to mean the will of the State, of

Figure 12.1 Figure of wood, glass beads. fibre and gold, Baule, Côte d'Ivoire (*Photo: Franko Khoury, NMAfA, Washington, DC*)

central government towards the regions. I would also speak of 'political will' but looking at it in the other direction. When a people or a region asks for the creation of a museum, that, in my opinion, is a political act in the strong sense of the term. And the example of the Eotile is enlightening. The creation of a museum is simply one means resorted to out of a determination to preserve their culture in the face of the onslaughts of a changing world, over which they have no control, in the face of State, economic and other power.

Eotile country today has more incomers living there than Eotile. The same moreover is true of the neighbouring region of Bonoua, where the Abouré have already built a museum to their culture. These are prosperous regions where economic development has drawn in workers from all over the country and from many neighbouring countries, and of course these workers have brought their own culture with them. From the viewpoint of a historian or a sociologist these regions can be looked at as models or microcosms of modern Côte d'Ivoire.

But what are we witnessing in both cases? We are witnessing the call for the creation of a local museum emanating from the group that is the historic owner of the land or the lagoons, a group which feels itself threatened by factors over which it has little control, different as between the two regions, and which feels the need to assert its rights, sometimes so as not to die, not by facing up to today's reality but by parading an image.

Should we conjure up the spectre of what may be the greatest danger about some conceptions of local museums? A conception of these museums that simply responded to particular local interests. An egotistic assertion of particularisms and interests that no longer correspond to the actual society. A schizophrenic view of things which, associated with real problems of cultural (and sometimes economic) survival might be a real danger to a national unity that is often still very fragile.

Note 1. See J. Polet, 'Sondages archéologiques en pays Eotilé: Assoco–Monobaha–Belibete–Nyamwan', *Bulletin de l'IHAAA* 2 (1976), pp. 121–39; *id.*, 'Archéologie d'une région lagunaire: le pays Eotilé', *Recherche, pédagogie et culture* 55 (1981), pp. 52-5.

13 Community Initiative & National Support at the Asante Cultural Centre • Ghana

FRANCIS BOAKYE DUAH

Ghana National Cultural Centre which is a community initiative and national support is concerned with a multi-purpose cultural institution. The buildings of the centre are based on a building style that grew up, at some unknown date, in the forest region of Ghana.

The Asante are a people of Akan stock whose oral traditions claim both that they originated north of the forest belt and also that they came from the area of Adansi, immediately to the south of the territory which they now occupy. Whatever their earlier history, it is probable that Kumasi and certain nearby towns were founded early in the seventeenth century by people from Adansi in order to control the main trade routes which led from the gold and kola-producing forest region northward to the Sudan. Towards the end of the seventeenth century, they were forged into a powerful confederacy by Osei Tutu of Kumasi, who was made Asantehene, ruler of Asante. Osei Tutu's chief priest and adviser, Okomfo Anokye, gave spiritual authority to the new regime by creating the Golden Stool of Asante, symbolising the soul of the Asante nation.

The Asantes, who number over two million (1984: 2,090,100) occupy an area of 24,389 km². It is densely forested. And because of the richness of forest land in soil, mineral and vegetable products, the region is renowned as the richest in the country.

Figure 13.1 **Asante musical instrument**
(*Photo: British Museum*)

Beginning of the Project

The Ghana National Cultural Centre sprang into existence with careful preparation, thanks to the foresight of the late Dr Alex Yaw Kyerematen – not a museum professional but a patron and a supporter of museums, monuments, historic sites and a promoter of cultures. Born on 29 April 1916, he left the then Gold Coast (Ghana) for

105

Figure 13.2 Asante musical instrument (*Photo: British Museum*)

Figure 13.3a Three Asante terracotta pots (*Photo: British Museum*)

Durham University in 1946 and proceeded to Oxford University. While in the United Kingdom he realised that there was an urgent need for the preservation of Ghana's cultural and natural heritage, not only in writing but in such concrete forms as museums, zoos, archives, theatres, craft centres for indigenous Ghanaian craftsmen, traditional music and dancing groups, drama groups and even a library where books about our arts and culture could be made readily available to any aspiring Ghanaian who wanted to learn more about them or research further into them. By the time he returned to the Gold Coast in 1950, Dr Kyerematen had drawn up a comprehensive programme of activities aimed at putting life into this mental picture and getting it off the ground. He succeeded in enlisting the enthusiasm and support of most of his friends and other influential personalities in Kumasi. Everyone he approached sounded very friendly and outwardly sympathetic but nothing beyond that.

It was at this stage that Dr Kyerematen approached the late Otumfuor Sir Osei Agyeman Prempeh II, Asantehene, who gave him support, inspiration and blessing. At its meeting on 5 July 1951 the Asanteman Council appointed a committee, with the following terms of reference: 'To make recommendations to the Council on the steps to be taken for the establishment of a centre whose functions will include the preservation of Asante culture, the fostering of social research and the publication of a newsletter and a journal containing notes on Asante customs and other matters of general interest'.

Figure 13.3b Close-up of central
terracotta pot
(*Photo: British Museum*)

A building committee was accordingly appointed. To make it broad-based, the committee included representatives of the Asanteman Council, the Kumasi State Council, the then Ministry of Education and Social Welfare, the then University College of the Gold Coast, the then Kumasi College of Technology, the British Council, the National Museum of Ghana, the Ghana Library Board, the then Kumasi Chamber of Commerce, the then Lebanese community, the then Syrian community, the Zongo community, the Asante Kotoko Society and the Asante Youth Association. It is worth nothing that among the specialists welcomed at some of its meetings were Dr and Mrs M.J. Herskovits, well known Africanists and anthropologists.

The first building to be put on the site was the library. It was put up by the Ghana Library Board and was opened to the public in July 1954. Although it forms part of the centre, the library is owned and controlled by the Library Board. The Archives building was next to be completed.

The real projects started and completed by the centre's building committee include the zoo, which occupies an area of twenty-eight

Projects completed to date

107

Figure 13.4 The Ashanti library
(Photo: Duah)

acres. It was designed by George Cansdale, then Superintendent of the London Zoo; it is now owned and controlled by the Department of Game and Wild Life. An exhibition hall known as Independence Exhibition Hall and an ornamental drinking water fountain were erected in 1958. There are also a Made-in-Ghana Goods Exhibition Hall, a theatre and dance arena (Dwabe remkumaa) and a craft gallery and bazaar. The Patakesee, a simple but well constructed hall which accommodates well over 2,000 persons, is used for concerts, piano recitals, plays, and drumming and dancing, committee meetings, public

Figure 13.5 Ornamental fountain with four state swords, symbolising the fight for freedom
(Photo: Duah)

Figure 13.6 The Patakesee
(*Photo: Duah*)

lectures and examinations. Within its precincts are bars and a canteen.

From the very beginning of the centre's history, the planners conceived the idea of a chapel to represent contemporary religion, which was completed in 1959. Next to the open-air chapel is the oratory, dedicated to the memory of the late Asantehene, Otumfuor Sir Osei Agyeman Prempeh II, and all the founding members of the centre who have departed this life. There is also an imposing building of considerable architectural beauty named after one of the founding members, Mr Quashie-Idun.

Figure 13.7 The Oratory
(*Photo: Duah*)

109

Figure 13.8 The Anokye Komaam (*Photo: Duah*)

Figure 13.9 Part of the façade of the museum (*Photo: Duah*)

The Anokye Komaam, or shrine, represents Ghanaian traditional religion. The first apartment is reserved for drummers (Akyeremadefoo), who provide music for dancing for the priest. Next to this comes a bath, a kitchen and a sleeping room for the priest. There is also a reconstructed village, comprising cocoa farm, poultry farm, graveyard, food crop farm, palm wine booth and so on.

The first real project to be started by the centre's building committee was a museum, named after the late Asantehene Otumfuor Sir Osei Agyeman Prempeh II, the Prempeh II Jubilee Museum to commemorate his twenty-five years on the Golden Stool. It was designed in four phases, the first of which was completed at a cost of nearly 20,000 cedis and was opened on 27 October 1956 by the Asantehene himself.

The completed first phase is an exhibit in itself, since it represents the architectural form of a traditional Asante chief's house. The façade and the inner walls are richly adorned with traditional sculptural motifs made by Harold Cox of the Slade School of Art, London, in reconstructed stone cast out of plaster moulds of traditional wall decorations. Within the courtyard flourishes an Edwene tree (*Baphia Nitida*), the Akan symbolic tree of wisdom. This replica of a traditional house, built in contemporary materials to ensure a long lease of life, is set in a paved courtyard. Along the sides of the paved courtyard and at the edges of the house are grass plots on which are grown a variety of indigenous trees, plants and cacti to support the atmosphere in which the Asante traditional culture has stood for centuries.

Figure 13.10 Courtyard displaying drums, the 'Edwene tree' and a typical Asante kitchen (*Photo: Duah*)

Among the objects of historical significance is the silver-plated stool of Nana Ntim Gyakari, King of the Denkyira, once lord of the Asantes. This king was sitting on this stool playing the game of ware (*mankala*) with his wife at Feyiase, a village then eight miles from Kumasi, during his campaign against the Asante for rebelling against him (about 1700). Caught unawares during the game, he was slain and his army routed.

One of the rooms of the museum is devoted to musical instruments, such as drums, horns, flutes, gong-gongs, stringed instruments and rattles. There are several items of regalia, most of them brought back from Britain during Queen Elizabeth's visit to Ghana. Okomfo Anokye's treasure box, believed to contain certain valuables but not to not be opened. It has never, in fact, been opened or x-rayed. There is a brass pan popularly known as the Brass Pan of Independence which caused the Asantes' revolt against the Denkyiras in the seventeenth century. At the moment, the objects at the museum are mostly from Asante chiefs.

Figure 13.11 State chairs on display (*Photo: Duah*)

111

*The structure, organisation
& administration
of the centre*

The centre, therefore, can be said to be a real folk museum, an open-air museum and, better still, a cultural complex.

The cultural centre in Kumasi, it is argued, is a regional cultural centre. This type of project has already proved a big success in Niger, Tanzania and Zambia, to mention only a few countries. The late President Nkrumah nationalised the centre and named it the Ghana National Cultural Centre in 1963. Since it is the aim of the government of Ghana to establish multi-purpose cultural centres throughout the regional capitals and district headquarters, it will be no more than appropriate if the Kumasi centre reverts to its former name – Asante Cultural Centre.

The Kumasi project, we can say, provides a unique opportunity of demonstrating the doctrine of self-help which is so vital to the young countries of Africa, with many developmental schemes to attend to and advantages to be derived from all sections of the community working together for the common good.

The spadework and the moving spirit behind the centre involved just a handful of selfless and devoted individuals like Dr Alex Atta Yaw Kyerematen, who took the initiative. Today the centre has become purely local and is responsive to community needs. The Kumasi or Asante community decided for itself that it wanted a cultural centre, rather than having a central administration, or some entity outside the community deciding that it would be nice to create a cultural centre or local museum for them.

In fact, let us reflect on the general title we have given this chapter: 'Community Initiative and National Support at the Asante Cultural Centre'. The prosperity of a local museum is by the people, of the people and for the people. In short, Ghana needs a museological policy wisely formulated.

14 *The Prefectorial Museum at Boké • Guinea*

SORY KABA

The prefecture of Boké is situated on the northern edge of the Guinean coastline and covers an area of some 11,054 km². It is bordered on the north by Guinea-Bissau, on the south by the prefecture of Boifa, on the east by the prefecture of Télimélé and to the west by the Atlantic Ocean along a 53 km coast. The population of Boké, estimated at 180,000, is made up mainly of farmers and herdsmen. The dominant groups are the Landouma, Baga, Nalu, Mikhifore, Tanda, Yola and Fulbe, in addition to whom there are a few Soso, Balante (Kanfarandé, Sarakolé and Diakhanké (central Boké)). The prefecture of Boké contains significant cultural and natural riches.

The prefecture of Boké

Figure 14.1a & b Front and rear views of carved wooden drum in form of kneeling woman holding a child and bearing a ring of six masks, Baga, Guinée
(*Photo: British Museum*)

113

The prefectorial museum of Boké was created as a result of circular No. 258/MDI March 1971; it also houses the prefecture's archives lodged in a small fort, built in 1978, and is regarded as the chief historical monument in the prefecture. The museum was restored and equipped, at a total cost of some 1,140,000 sylis, through the combined action of the prefectorial authorities and the Club des amis du musée de Boké (CAMB). It was officially opened on 6 June 1982.

Figure 14.2 Heddle pulley, Guinée (*Photo: British Museum*)

The museum occupies a two-storey building: the ground floor is devoted to exhibitions, while the first floor is given over to the prefecture's archives and the museum offices. The cellar is empty at present, but colonial pieces will be put there.

The current exhibition displays mainly ethnographic items; sculptures (masks, statuettes), ritual objects, objects associated with public ceremonies (marriage, baptism, circumcision), musical instruments, traditional weapons and hunting gear. A few colonial items are on display.

The current situation

In order to give greater impetus to the museum so that it meets the demands of a cultural and document institution better, a programme has been embarked on which combines:

1. The formation of a prefectorial support group for the museum which is chaired by the prefect and has the task of promoting museum activity in the prefecture, collecting funds and organising an annual cultural week to support the museum,

2. The creation of a prefectorial commission responsible for scientific research and documentation which will co-ordinate all research activities in the prefecture,

3. The publication of an information bulletin, *Le Kakilambe*,

4. The help of the Club des amis du musée de Boké: set up in 1981 by expatriates in Kamsar and Songarédi; it has as its aims to support the activities of the museum, organise a craft centre and lay out a botanical garden in the museum courtyard.

Relaunching the museum

15 *The Regional Museums at Gao & Sikasso • Mali*

Two case studies will be presented here, of the museums at Gao and Sikasso. On 17 and 18 May 1976 two 'study days on museums and heritage' were held in Bamako which marked a decisive turning-point in the history of museums in Mali, as they led to the setting out of a museum policy and the drafting of a proposal for establishing regional and local museums. It was in implementation of this programme that the project for a *musée régional* at Gao got under way in 1980 and for one at Sikasso in 1983.

The story of these two experiences deserves telling because the mistakes made in the first case enabled us to correct the way we went about establishing the regional museum at Sikasso.

The regional museum at Gao, or the Musée du Sahel

In 1980, following ecological changes in northern Mali, the idea of organising an exhibition to draw attention to the tragedy in the Sahel gained ground among officials in the Ministry of Culture. It was intended to serve as the inaugural exhibition of the Musée du Sahel.

The first collection was realised in 1980, based on financing by the Overseas Museum in Bremen. It was also with the technical and conceptual help of the same museum that an exhibition on the Sahel was mounted in Gao in November 1981. The exhibition signalled the take-off of the museum. Next, a second collection, financed hy the United States embassy in Mali, was put together. These two collections were stored in a dwelling house in Gao with small rooms which was to serve as a temporary museum.

The museum's immediate environment does not provide very suitable conditions for the proper conservation of the collections. The

116

museum building is situated in a residential area, with private dwellings on either side. The pollution from household activities (smoke, dust and other dirt) is harmful to the conservation of items, especially as the bulk of the collections is made up of leather objects and woven leaf mats. The building itself has major disadvantages. Although the risk of objects being stolen is slight, the existence of two entrances – aligned on an east–west axis – when the museum has only a single guard indicates that security measures need to be improved. The conditions of the lease rule out any use of the walls for fixing supports for exhibits or shelves, and so the possibility of making maximum use of the space available for exhibiting and storing collections is very limited.

For the Gao museum, as for any other cultural institution, the need to put down roots in the local communities is vital. Although stress ought to have been laid on these aspects long before the launching of the project, personnel changes, combined with the fact that the museum is a long way from where the decisions are made in Bamako, militated against effective co-ordination of project-related activities, not to mention the political incidents following the regional elections at the time of the inaugural exhibition. The preview of the inaugural exhibition, devoted to the Kel Adrar (Tamashek) nomads coincided with the declaration of the results of the elections, and the opening of the museum was seen as a celebration of the victory of the winning group – whose leader was of Tamashek origin over the losing group, with which the Sonrai, the settled inhabitants of the town of Gao, identified.

However, explanations by officials of the Ministry of Culture managed to satisfy both sides. It must be hoped that the series of educational programmes aimed at schools as well as contacts with local associations will lead to the museum becoming better integrated into its social environment.

Two major problems remain: the search for premises which will enable the museum to operate better and the training of local museum staff. In planning this training, it is proposed to organise basic training in museum techniques for personnel from the Gao museum at the Musée national. This experience taught us the important lesson that when a cultural institution like a museum is established without first securing the support of the local population, it ends up being rejected. The consciousness-raising activities embarked on at the time the project was launched proved insufficient. Hence the need once again to undertake sustained action to promote awareness among the local communities.

The project started in 1983. The experience at Gao, especially the mistakes that were made, was taken on board in deciding on the approach to the establishment of the regional museum at Sikasso. Given the difficulties encountered by the Musée du Sahel, and also in the absence of special funds for local museums, we tried other approaches, this time seeking support among the local communities. As regards the technical aspects of the project, the support of the Musée national was sought. From the very beginning the museum was planned with all these factors taken into account.

A very important fact was that since 1982 the proposal for a regional museum at Sikasso had been the subject of a local request by the mayor of the town of Sikasso. Following the first contacts made with leading regional figures, and at the request of the local authorities, the basic documents of the project were drawn up by a working group composed of technicians from the Musée national and the service co-ordinating local museum projects. This working group stressed the need to raise awareness among the local people, and for the Musée national to participate in the project and be a source of technical support in establishing the regional museum at Sikasso. This study proposed the following approach:

1. Setting out a minimum structure, starting from the principle that a local museum can take off on the basis of a very simple structure. This definition consisted in identifying working spaces, estimating areas needed immediately, laying out the broad outlines of the architectural programme, taking account of possibilities for extension, the architectural style, conservation problems, etc.

2. Planning museum activities at the time when the museum is established. This planning concerned the collection and processing of objects, the basic training of technical personnel and the mounting of the inaugural exhibition.

3. Follow-up and technical supervision of the regional museum at Sikasso. It was felt that, as there was no general inspectorate of museums, this work could be carried out by the services of the Musée national.

Such are the main points of this study, which continues to guide the project for setting up a regional museum at Sikasso. The first collection has already been put together, thanks to financing from the Ford Foundation, obtained through the good offices of WAMP. It has already been processed in the Musée national.

It is perhaps still premature to call Sikasso a museum since it has not yet opened its doors. Yet when it is considered that a collection is already in existence, and that a person has been appointed to run the museum and is currently undergoing training at the Musée national du Mali, there are grounds for optimism. But the great concern at the moment is the search for temporary premises suitable for museum activities. The local population are in favour of the search for and acquisition of such premises. It also envisaged that the costs of building the local museum will be paid by the people of Sikasso.

16 *The Proposed Eco-Museum at Ziguinchor • Senegal*

PAPE TOUMANI NDIAYE

This chapter is simply the highly theoretical presentation of a proposal for an eco-museum in the course of creation at Ziguinchor.

The starting point Ziguinchor, the chief urban centre in Casamance, is a town without a socio-cultural structure. Casamance can be described as the Guinean-Sudanese zone of Senegal. It is watered by the river of the same name. It is inhabited by an ethnic mosaic of which the most important components are the Fula, the Sossé (or Mandinka) and the Diola. The town of Ziguinchor has a population of some 80,000.

Given the lack of cultural infrastructure, a need appeared among the population. The idea of a museum or eco-museum began to take hold, and several proposals were put forward by several quite unrelated individuals. The merit of the present project is to open up to the others, break the isolation and organise co-operation.

On the ground, things are not simple. Casamance is experiencing a gradual decline in rainfall. This situation arouses existential anguish among the population. Unconsciously, some of them see it as an eschatalogical sign arising from a cosmic disorder.

It is in fact rather difficult to put one's finger on a cultural image that a society forms of itself. To do so is to touch the consciousness of a community. In managing community relations one is managing the collective spirit and imagination. Hence the idea of a community museum which would promote solidarity, at the same time as being an outcome of the anguish, since it would have as its mission to explain the deterioration of the climate while taking on the cultural heritage.

1. *Illustration of traditions of soil conservation and the protection of biological settlements*. This is to show how earlier generations were concerned to exploit the riches of nature, while caring for them. This objective is part and parcel of the fight against desertification and loss of livestock.

2. *The ecology of pollution caused by man*, in relation to safeguarding the beauties of nature. This point stresses the multiple dangers of human activities: water and atmospheric pollution by industrial waste, deforestation by bush fires and uncontrolled felling of trees, uncontrolled hunting and fishing.

3. *Protection of genetic variety* and keeping alive the possibility of studying nature. It is a matter of attracting attention to the disappearance of a number of vegetable and animal species whose existence is necessary to the equilibrium of eco-systems. This objective aims also to ensure access to the study of nature as man's privileged biological environment.

4 *History, geography and culture*, in short; the aim is to show the place of the region in the Senegalese nation, and the historical, geographical, cultural and political foundations of that position.

Figure 16.1 Two figures, Bissagos Is., Guinea-Bissau (*Photo: British Museum*)

121

5. *Rediscovering the cultural heritage* through the creation of a network of people to collect and acquire material and non-material evidence. Permanent or temporary exhibitions, fixed or travelling, would be organised, using national and international languages, to guarantee that all have access to knowledge. Tours would be structured in such a way as to stimulate and reinforce curiosity and capture the attention.

6. *Use of local techniques and know-how to promote a rebirth of crafts.* The existence of traditional trades is marked by repetitive production destined for tourist consumption, while industrial substitution products are often unsuitable. The intention is not to freeze traditional trades, but to focus attention on adapting them to the environment which gave them being and the need for their transformation, given the evolution of that environment.

7. *Educational activity?* The first approach would be to promote the formation of an association with the job of breathing life into the museum by using and updating tales, legends and myths, as well as folklore. Visits by school groups and youth workshops would be organised regularly.

Figure 16.2a & b Details of front and back of textile, from upper Senegal (see also Figure 1.2) (*Photo: British Museum*)

8. *Observation of changes*. A team of representatives of the various research areas (natural heritage, cultural heritage, etc.) would be created with a view to analysing the changes under way, so as to turn them into topics for papers or exhibitions.

Those in charge would be called on to draw up questionnaires to sound out public opinion and assess the results of the institution. This would be one of the means of correcting errors, so as to meet the expectations of visitors and the people, which is the major concern.

In conclusion, it must be observed that the above objectives raise a series of questions. How to reconcile respect and knowledge? How to accept a large number of visitors without such openness meaning alienation and deterioration? How to give priority to the interests of the people, since it is on them that the life of the region depends, while at the same time providing for those of visitors? How to organise a dialogue between the two categories of partners, knowing that for part

Measures of effectiveness in relation to objectives set

of the population the visitor is a source of profit, and for the rest he remains an outsider? In the light of all these questions there emerges on the one hand the usefulness of being able to communicate what it is that is original and rich in the natural and cultural heritage of Casamance. And from that arises the concern to defend it and the need for information to come principally from the people of Casamance themselves, through a dialogue around and within the institution. between this population and its guests. It is thus with the idea of promoting and developing that exchange that the hospitality and educational programme of the institution would have to be drawn up.

Figure 16.3 Heddle pulley, Senoufo, Côte d'Ivoire (*Photo: British Museum*)

124

17 *The Situation of Museums in Togo*

MOUSSA MADJABABA TCHANILE

Togo is a modest-size country, with a population of 3 million. It experienced the rule of three foreign powers – the Germans, the British and the French – who diverted the country from its original evolution by imposing on it their own cultures. But it has been able to retain its own cultures, which today, with the country's authenticity policy, constitutes the priceless treasure of its national cultural heritage.

We say too that the cultural policy pursued by the party – that is, the Togolese People's Rally – and the government has enabled all classes of the population to put an end to this 'ethnophagy'. And this new awareness of customs and traditions has enabled Togo to have a *musée national*. Some towns, such as Aného (in the prefecture of Lacs), Notsé (in the prefecture of Hano) and Sokode (in the prefecture of Tchaoudjo) are currently being provided with local museums.

It is worth pointing out that the term 'museum' was absent from the Togolese cultural vocabulary before the advent of the Eyadema regime. Whereas most formerly colonised African countries had inherited at least a so-called conventional museum before attaining independence, in Togo all one can point to is a few initiatives which unfortunately were still-born. Thus, during the German occupation, in 1906, the intention was expressed of establishing a *Land-Museum*, that is, a museum of the country. After Germany, it was France's turn through the agency of the Institut Français d'Afrique Noire (IFAN), to promote museum activity in Togo, as in other French colonies.

Despite all these initiatives, the museum problem was posed concretely only in 1975, the year of the inauguration of the Musée national, the very first of its type in Togo. The Musée national was established on 8 April 1974 by decree of the President of the Republic. The whole Togolese people rejoiced at this institution, on which falls

125

the task of conserving the material culture of the country. And, as a member of the government said, 'The museum constitutes an important link in the chain of natural cultural policy.' That well reflects the awareness on the part of the government of the problems of conserving and preserving the country's cultural property. Moreover, the creation of the Musée national in Lomé was followed by the inauguration of a regional museum at Kara in November 1982.

Togo, then, now has museums, and it is up to those in charge of museums to make all social classes aware of them so that each Togolese feels concerned by the problems of preserving and conserving the national cultural heritage. That is what led us in 1980 to embark on a policy of raising the people's awareness, especially in the rural areas, which are generally the areas where objects that have museum potential are held.

Consciousness-raising policy

When it met political, administrative and traditional leaders, the consciousness-raising team dealt with points such as the museum and its contribution to the country's development and the building and consolidation of national unity. The aim was to promote understanding of the important role that a museum is called upon to play in a developing country such as ours.

The first tour took place in the latter half of 1980 throughout the country. The second was in the Kara region, which covers six prefectures. It was more productive than the first one, because the team was able to survey and collect cultural property immediately in some prefectures where the idea of a museum took on quickly.

In 1984 the Direction du Musée national, des sites et monuments attempted another form of consciousness-raising by a travelling exhibition on the theme 'The museum and the public'. This exhibition was shown in several towns in the country and had as its main aim to show that the objects that the museum collects from time to time from their custodians are never lost and are kept in good condition, with the aim of serving the people culturally and historically.

Although this exhibition has not yet visited every region of the country, the Direction du Musée has already recorded encouraging results. At Aného (one of the oldest towns in Togo and its first capital), for example, at the request of the population, the exhibition stayed two months longer than planned.

Consciousness-raising among schoolchildren is based on demonstrations and talks organised mainly during school cultural weeks, which occur every year during the second term. In addition the Direction du Musée national organises guided tours for primary schoolchildren. We feel this method is insufficient, since it benefits only children in the capital. That points to the need to develop local museums with the aim of giving the same opportunity to young people in other parts of the country. While awaiting the establishment of local, or, failing that, regional museums, we have thought of travelling exhibitions in the large towns. As for children in remote villages, we are considering organising travel for them to visit the museum, in co-operation with the teachers in those areas.

Consciousness-raising among adults. We have tried, whenever possible, to organise meetings bringing old people and young ones together in towns and villages. Another means has been the use of the mass media. Articles on museums have been published in *La Nouvelle Marche* (daily), the review *Togo-Dialogue* and *Bingo*. There have also been programmes on the radio.

Since 1983 the Direction du Musée national has endeavoured successfully to train young people through study days and national training and consciousness-raising seminars in collaboration with the Fondation Eyadema, aimed at staff and officials in the Ministry of Youth, Sports and Culture, and other departments such as National Education and Tourism. The topics of these seminars were:

Museum policy in Togo.

Museums and development.

The problem of the looting and illicit transfer of cultural property.

Means of acquiring museum items.

Promoting appreciation of museum items through exhibitions.

Museums and tourism.

The role of oral tradition in the collection of museum items.

The problem of collecting and documenting museum items.

The topics are dealt with either by museum staff and officials or by invited individuals from other sections in the Department of Cultural Affairs and Tourism.

Generally speaking, despite the difficulties, information on museums and their role has reached most of the population of Togo, who have proved to be a receptive audience.

Museum visits. There has been a great shift in the pattern of museum attendance at the Musée national. It used to be that only foreigners and students visited the museum regularly. Only a few adult nationals – barely seventy – were recorded as entering the museum each month. In 1983 this same museum recorded an annual average of 200 adult national visitors, but 198 between January and March 1985. In addition, the Musée national receives many pupils from towns and villages in other parts of the country, who put their holidays to good use by getting to know items in museums. It should also be noted that officials and traditional authorities from other towns also sometimes pay for the journey to come and visit the museum that they have heard about.

Regional museum and proposed museums in prefectures. The consciousness-raising campaigns conducted in 1983 created among the people a sort of pride in having a museum in their home town or prefecture at any price. Less then ten years ago they would have opposed any collection of objects, not wanting to give up their cultural property. Today almost everyone expresses the desire to see a museum come into being in his area. In some towns the idea of creating a museum has already become reality. At Aného premises are being laid out to house the region's Musée d'histoire et ethnographie and the collection of old objects has begun.

While it is true that museum activities and policy are proceeding well, we must deplore some negative factors.

Since 1975 the Musée national has remained at an embryonic stage in a space in the House of the Togolese People's Rally. This space, consisting of a large exhibition hall, a corridor also used for exhibition displays and a cellar, had been set aside as a temporary home for the national museum until the Musée vivant could be built. Unfortunately, this latter has remained at the project stage, the premises selected not being large enough to accommodate the various sections which it should normally have.

We must also stress the inadequacy of means of transport. The Musée national is the central museum and must therefore co-ordinate the activities of the other museums, help them to acquire their collections and organise cultural activities.

The Musée national has remained in this state for ten years, perhaps because it was still young and unknown to the general public, the scientific community and regional and international bodies.

We feel that, starting from the Lomé meeting, contacts and relations will be established between the Musée national of Togo and international agencies and museum professionals and that we shall be able to benefit from our respective experiences.

Index

131